THE
PARENT
AGENT

*How to represent your child and get them
into the college of their choice*

By Verdel Jones

PARAMIND PUBLICATIONS
A *Shift* in Thinking

ParaMind Publications

Copyright © 2016 by Verdel Jones
Published by ParaMind Publications

Editor: Marti Covington

Library of Congress Control Number: 2016903864
ISBN 978-0-9762738-6-8
Printed in the United States of America

Dedication

To my family, thank you for supporting me and always having my back. Every day I wake up in gratitude, in awe of the unconditional love I receive. You are the best part of me.

Contents

#FAMILY
12/2011

To
Heather + Todd

Thank you so
much for you
Support! I Love
you guys!

#FAMILY

UD A Se
10/2016

Introduction

My Personal and Professional Experience Sending Students to College

● ●

This Book Should Help You Understand:

▶ Why You want to be Your Child's Parent Agent

▶ What it Takes to Be a Successful Parent Agent

▶ When to Be a Parent and When to be an Agent

● ●

AGENT POV:

Each chapter will provide an Agent POV to help you see the situation from an agents point of view

PARENT POV:

Each chapter will provide a Parent POV to help you see the situation from your own point of view as a parent

"Knowledge is power. Information is liberating. Education is the premise of progress, in every society, in every family."

~Kofi Annan

*E*very parent has an 'Aha!' moment as they raise children. Mine came when I thought of what I had done, in the life of each child, to get them into college. As I reviewed everything that had to happen to help them get accepted into their preferred institutions of higher learning, I realized something important. I had become an agent. Now let me explain what that means. Agents exist in big dollar competitive industries to get the best deals for their clients. In sports, an agent negotiates with team owners to get the most money for a player. Agents who represent actors or directors want their clients to have the biggest and best-paying projects. Good agents find great opportunities and then make sure their clients receive them.

If you successfully become a Parent/Agent, you'll know it, because you'll feel like you helped build a brand. Getting my last child off to college was a rewarding feeling. But that wasn't my only emotion. I was simultaneously, exhausted, sad, excited and proud. We drove to the college, helped my incoming freshman unload and started the trip home as empty nesters. Yes, it was hard to see my youngest child go. The ride seemed extremely long as my husband attempted to take my mind off the fact that my last baby had just left.

After all, we knew this day would come and we were as prepared as we could be. It helped that I had been here before with my son. However, I also had the benefit of helping thousands of other students do the exact same thing during my years in education. What aided us tremendously during the college seek, find and fund process was knowing how to define roles. I knew from experience that you can't assume who will do what. A good Parent/Agent assigns tasks, otherwise you can watch coveted opportunities slip through your fingers.

Why You Want to be your Child's Parent/Agent

Simply put, a parent representing a child's quest to get into college acts as the middlemen between that child and the child's choice of a higher learning institution. A Parent/Agent helps his or her child make college decisions that provide the best chance of developing success. I did that by looking for ways to help my children grow and develop. I wanted my children to get the best deal possible on the team (college) of their choice. I came to understand that is no different than what sports or entertainment agents want for the people they represent. A good agent goes beyond basic contract negotiations. They also work out marketing, speaking and entertainment deals. When you talk to a successful agent, you might learn that they selected that vocation because they love sports or movies and want to see talented participants get the best chances to develop their craft. Well, I love my children and love working out the best opportunities for them, just like a good agent.

The more I thought about it, the more I saw other similarities. Young athletes and aspiring big-name actors are a lot like your soon-to-be college student. All have to make tough choices about changing their status. Actors, directors and athletes want to move from amateur to professional status. Your child plans to make the transition from high school to college. Everyone has different reasons that motivate them. The professionals in entertainment and sports may want an agent so they can realize a dramatic increase in pay. But your child may want to attend college because of what they expect to happen after they graduate. In both cases, goals have to be discussed because those goals are a catalyst for developing a game plan.

I understand professionally how important a good game plan is because for the last twenty-two years I've championed this course of action in a New York State school district as a District Director of Guidance & Support Services. That means I supervise all the school counselors, social workers and nurses in a number of schools. It's my job to make sure we have programs that accomplish two objectives. First, we have to satisfy the needs of the community. But my job is also to provide the resources the counselors need to help our students transition into colleges and universities. I develop programs such as college nights, SAT preparation workshops or financial aid seminars to help both students and parents understand some of the concepts discussed in this book. I'm passionate about this topic, so I also organize formal and informal sessions that can help parents and students understand what courses are appropriate to take in high school.

My goal is to give young people tools that allow them to excel. It helps that I have spent three years of my professional educational career as a school counselor. That perspective, combined with my interaction with college recruiters and, of course, my experience as a mother, helps me write the information you're reading. It's also why I will provide many details, personal observations and lists. If you want to successfully navigate the college application process you have to make and execute long range plans in addition to being organized. I warn you now, that means making and checking off the items on a lot of lists.

What it Takes to Be a Successful Parent/Agent

But before working on your child, you may have to work on you. You see, I believe the first fact you have to process as a Parent/ Agent is that your personal aspirations are not important. You are doing this to help your children realize dreams that will make them productive and happy. It requires forming a team and your children are active participants. Actually, the formation of that team takes place during a child's formative years. In my case, it involved a two parent household. However, I can list hundreds of success stories and each is different from the other.

A successful Parent/Agent knows that grades alone will not help a student get accepted into the college of his or her choice. Good grades are important, but they are not the only factor.

College decision makers want students who understand the components of living a balanced life. In my family, I put on my agent hat to guide my children so they would get involved in programs that took place not only in school, but out of school as well. The goal was to expose them to leadership opportunities. I continued to wear my hat as their agent when I researched which opportunities to choose. But I had to put my parent hat back on when it came time to make those choices.

The ultimate goal for me as the Parent/Agent for my children was to get them admitted to a college or university that would help them become the adults that I had hoped to raise. I wanted them to do well. The reward for me is not just monetary. I want to see them happy, thriving, healthy and doing something they love. If a check comes with that at some point, I'll take that too. However, I caution everyone who builds a Parent/Agent and client/student team to understand one fact. Many of the most lucrative careers in 2015 didn't exist ten years ago. The first iPhone was released in 2007. Young people in college at that time could not prepare to work in a technology that would revolutionize the world, but they could develop skills that would allow them to gain employment as the world became more digital. The trick for the Parent/Agent is not to exert control based on what you think you know, because sadly, that information may become outdated far sooner than you could expect.

If you can't plan the future based on past experience and educational trends how do you guide your child toward a successful choice in college? It's a difficult question to answer which is why I decided to share what has worked for me as well as the thousands I've helped matriculate through my district. I'm now excited to share this process with you. My hope is that the information presented in these pages is used to get more of our children prepared to, not only attend college, but attend the one of their choice.

When to Be a Parent and When to be an Agent

A good Parent/Agent has to constantly be aware of emotions. You have to recognize that graduating from high school and heading toward college is difficult for your teen. You also have to be gentle with yourself as you hurdle toward this major milestone in your own life. Still, this transition from high school to college is not something that can be made with a light-hearted approach. You will find yourself switching between the duties of being a good parent and being a good agent with lightning speed. But when you wear the hat of an agent you have to stay focused. You are securing college entrance for your child the same way an agent places a young actor in a very visible part on screen or the agent of a minor league ball player offers scouts from larger organizations a chance to see his client practice.

Sports and entertainment agents benefit financially by receiving a percentage of the contract they help their clients to secure. Parent/Agents receive a different type of payment and it is something money can't buy. Parent/Agents are rewarded when their children successfully navigate their way to a college degree and then begin their lives as adults.

Throughout the pages of this book I will tell you about the sense of accomplishment I have and had as a Parent/Agent for my own children. Both were accepted to excellent academic institutions that were appropriate and offered the programs needed to set them up for success in the future.

It is now my time to watch them shine on their road to establishing careers of their choice.

By now you have realized that if you want to become a great Parent/Agent for your child, there are a few personality traits and skill sets you'll have to develop. I'll discuss what has worked for me and thousands of other parents throughout the course of this book. But the most important trait is staying focused on what matters. It will be easy to get side-tracked, in fact expect it from your teen and even yourself. You, however, have to remain clear-headed. Your objective is to get the acceptance letter from the college of your child's choice and all decisions you make should support that goal. You will also have a secondary goal. It centers around paying for college. I discuss that in detail later in the book. But beyond the goals you will find a lot of joy as you find ways to unlock secrets about your child's personality that will ultimately make them something more than a successful college student.

The Parent Agent

How to represent your child and get them into the college of their choice

Chapter One

Goals to Set for Yourself as a Parent Agent

* *

This chapter will help you set goals:

▶ When to Start Laying the Foundation

▶ What to Notice about Your Child's Aptitude, Study Habits and Abilities

▶ Things to do BEFORE High School Classes Start

▶ Early College Research

▶ Developing the Skill of Long-range Time Management

▶ The Finance Talk

* *

AGENT POV:

Scout your children to know their strengths and weaknesses so you can develop an effective plan to leverage both.

PARENT POV:

You have to present multiple opportunities, because you don't know what will stick.

"Children must be taught how to think, not what to think."

~Margaret Mead

*A*s a Parent/Agent your role is to manage your child's academic career and help him or her get to a college of choice with the lowest out of pocket funds possible. A good Parent/Agent balances feelings of a parent who thinks 'That's my baby, I have to do whatever it takes to get my child prepared for and into college' with the professional agent attitude of, 'That's my client, and I don't win unless he/she does.' Your job is to provide both perspectives to help your student achieve college enrollment success. You need to start thinking like an agent by mentally making your child a first round draft choice or "A-lister." All of your decisions also have to include thoughts of LAC – Life After College, but more about that later.

The ongoing task of transforming into a Parent/Agent can be one of the biggest challenges in your life. This book is written to help explain the process and make it as simple as possible.

When to Start Laying the Foundation

Before you can set goals for your child, you need to reach them for yourself. Here are some ideas to help you take control of the process and achieve your ultimate objective; which is, get your student into college despite all the challenges and obstacles involved.

PREPPING YOUR STUDENT: IDEA #1:

Make Sure Your Student Knows That You Have Their Best Interest in Mind at All Times.

Your child needs to know that you wear two hats and have their back as a parent and an agent. As you probably have realized, things have changed since you were in school. Competition has become astronomically fierce for entrance into many colleges and the cost of higher education has skyrocketed.

Once I started doing research, I realized I had an immediate responsibility. I had to drive the vehicle which would lead my children into the college that was right for them. Your children have to know you are their advocate and prepared to help them get where they want to go. But there's something else you must do. You have to clear the road and that means watching for challenges or obstacles that might derail your child's chances for getting into the college of his or her choice.

PREPPING YOUR STUDENT: IDEA #2
Make Yourself Available. Schedule Time to Help Them.

One of the crucial components in this whole process revolves around time. You're going to have to find more of it. In fact, you're going to have to schedule time to help your college bound child. This process can't be done it spurts. We all know it can be hard enough to get ourselves prepared for events in our own lives. I understand from experience that the whole process of getting your student ready for college becomes exponentially harder, when you work outside of the home or have other children you're raising. But the steps needed to get your child into college are not ones that can be postponed or delayed. They're also too complicated for your child to execute alone. Your college bound child needs your help on a regular basis. So build a schedule for them, and as much as possible, stick to it.

PREPPING YOUR STUDENT: IDEA #3

Be Deliberate About What You Want to Achieve.

It is important to have clear intentions. You have to be specific about what you want and make sure your college bound student understands your specificity. Let me use myself as an example. I may have been a little overzealous at times, but I was deliberate. This can be a process of hurry up and wait. Your goal is to understand which deadlines and timelines are not forgiving compared to those that have some elasticity. For example, the deadlines for the SAT exam, college applications and scholarship submissions are absolute. You miss them and those opportunities are gone forever. However, you might be able to submit an additional recommendation or follow up essay after a posted deadline. You'll learn more about the perimeters of all these types of decisions later in this book What's important to remember is that you have to play to the part of an agent and stay the course until all documents are signed and your client/ student has the contract (college enrollment) of his or her choice.

PREPPING YOUR STUDENT: IDEA #4
You Must Serve as Their Guide.

Preparing your student for college is an involved process. It will require a lot of adult decisions. In many cases, you will be the most qualified person to make them. But don't take over the whole process because it can't be all about your plans without your college bound child's input. It takes time to understand all the roles and moving parts in the process. Part of your job as an agent is to help them learn the twists and turns of the college selection process with you. You also have to be a parent and stay far-sighted. Don't allow your child to focus on a popular choice, where all of his or her friends may attend. Instead, help them learn how to choose a school that will help them become who and what they desire to be. It is your job as a Parent/Agent to look for the type of institution that will foster what they have inside of them; to lead them into the career of their choice. It is also your job to help your child grow into the type of young person who can make an informed decision themselves.

My daughter didn't choose the college I was leaning toward, but I'm so happy she didn't listen to me because the college she chose was a perfect fit for the career she wanted to pursue. I'm glad she didn't allow me to persuade her to go somewhere else. You have to make sure your children are comfortable and secure in themselves to make the right decisions.

PREPPING YOUR STUDENT: IDEA #5

You Must Be Honest With Your Student In Addition to Encouraging Them.

This is a process that will help your child learn a lot about himself or herself. They will face rejection. They will get frustrated. They will feel that some aspects of the college selection process are unfair. Your job as a parent is to encourage them through all of these challenges. Your task as an agent is to be honest with them about their choices and limitations. The good news is that if you are simultaneously honest and encouraging you will lay a strong foundation for a trusting adult relationship.

It takes a little time to be able to do all this right. By time, I mean years. You need to develop game plans as a Parent/Agent that are executed all four years of high school - which can also be a very confusing time for your child.

One of the first facts you have to acknowledge is that you will need help to turn your plans into reality. This is the time an effective Parent/Agent seeks expert advice because this is something important. If you're like most parents, who don't do this all the time, you don't know what to ask. That's no reason for shame. You don't know what you don't know about this process. This fact alone makes it imperative to have that relationship with people such as your child's high school counselor. The counselor's role is to help guide you and your child on this journey toward college. The important fact you need to know is the information is available to you. Your job as a Parent/Agent is to find it. In turn, you will have better results in your search for the appropriate college for your child.

Professional agents help their clients navigate the often murky waters of their professional careers. A sports or music agent focuses on what their clients do well and concentrates on how to leverage that to achieve whatever level of success both client and agent can envision. If you want to become a successful Parent/Agent you will have to make a change in your thinking. You must carve out space or enlist help and support when you can. Identify a support team who can help you be the best Parent/Agent you can be.

College will have a major impact on your child's life, therefore we as Parent/Agents must do all we can to ensure it happens successfully. When I really began to think about myself as a Parent/Agent, I realized each of my children had to know that I was his or her advocate and prepared to help them get where they wanted to go.

What to Notice about Your Child's Aptitude, Study Habits and Abilities

Your children are not you. They are their own individuals and you must remember that as you start the process that will help them choose a college. Your children will pick up many of your traits but they also develop their own. As parents you have to honor that. As an effective Parent/Agent you have to look at the qualities they do have and encourage them. Don't make your children feel bad for not being like you. Once you understand the strengths that come with their individual personalities, you will be in a better position to represent them as a Parent/Agent.

You're looking for a scenario where you and your child will find the college that best fits their goals and desires. This is where knowing your child is crucial and once again, makes you wear two hats. What if your child is determined to be an Ivy League student, but hasn't earned the grades necessary to accomplish the goal? Then you have to wear your Agent hat and help them understand what can and can not happen. If your student has this dream, but has a 2.0 GPA in reality, the Ivy League is probably not for them, right now. You can also wear your Parent hat by letting them know that hope is not lost. But, there needs to be some realistic conversation about where they can go and what choices are available to them.

Quite frankly, you have to know a lot about your child before it's time to send out college application forms. Let me provide more personal examples.

My husband and I often talk about what our children like and don't like. We know our son's body language and can predict when he wants to ask a question. We've observed our daughter use a specific hand gesture when she is hiding something. We've learned that information by being observant, watching them and

Start talking with your children at an early age, hearing them and giving them the freedom of expression.

having constant dialogue. We let them know, while they were younger, that we wanted to hear their opinions.

It's imperative that you know your child. Why? Because a Parent/Agent must be able to motivate their client/student so you can point them in the right direction. The Agent knows his client's strengths and accentuates them. You, as your child's Agent, must do your research to determine the type of school that will help them showcase and use their interests and strengths to progress. This doesn't mean they will stay in one area for the rest of their lives, but interests or strengths help position them for adulthood.

How do you begin to learn who your child is? How do you find a program and then see if it's something that will hold their attention? It starts with talking with your children at an early age, hearing them and giving them the freedom of expression.

What does it mean to know your child and how does it affect the ability to search for a college? Well, even though I have assisted thousands of children get into college, the ones I know best are the two I raised. So, once again, I will use them as examples. I learned something about my son's style of learning from Sunday School. Let me explain. My mother would take the kids to Sunday School and she would say that my son, like most boys, seemed restless and not interested. However, when she would ask him questions about the lesson, he would quickly give an answer and share his perspective. The moral from this example? All children learn differently and Parent/Agents need to be aware of this.

Remember, I said the preparation for getting into college starts before high school and that you needed a team to help your child achieve the goal of college admission? Here's how that worked for our family. As I explained, we knew from observation the methodologies that helped our children learn. But keeping that information to ourselves didn't help them in classrooms and so we shared what we knew with our children's educators.

We wrote a letter every year, for both our children, to their teachers in elementary school and the guidance counselor in middle school. In the letter, we indicated how they best learned and what they liked. As mentioned earlier, our son might have looked like he daydreamed or goofed off in class but he still ingested and retained information. Our daughter loves to learn, write and read. However, she is a quiet person and it takes a while before she feels comfortable expressing herself. We helped their teachers get to know each child by writing those letters.

This approach was the first step toward helping our children get the most out of their education and be accepted into the colleges of their choice. But that was only possible because we truly knew them and the nuances that made them unique. I sincerely believed providing teachers and counselors with this information helped each educator understand the learning style for each of our children.

All of that notwithstanding, a good Parent/Agent should not oversell a child's abilities in any arena. A good Agent won't support someone who isn't committed to success. It is your job to match your child's talents with schools that will help those talents develop.

Both of my children have strong communication skills that they display in different ways. As a result, they attended colleges that met that interests. My son loves the movies. He would have been miserable if he had attended a college with no movie theaters close-by.   My daughter enjoys diversity and wanted to attend a college that could provide this.

Don't take this "knowing" for granted. If dialogue doesn't come easy to you, spend some time with your child discussing the questions below. You may get lucky and learn something about your child that you didn't know. Don't judge or ridicule any response. This is also a trust building exercise, but don't feel pressed to have them answer all these questions in one conversation. But do get all the answers and don't feel afraid to ask questions that aren't listed here.

Questions to help you get to know your child

- What is your favorite thing to do?

- What do you want to be when you grow up? Why?

- What is your favorite thing about school? Least favorite?

- Who is your hero? Why is this person a hero to you?

- If you could change one thing about yourself, what would it be?

- What are three things you do well?

- Describe something that really scares you.

- If you could visit any place in the world, where would it be?

- What is your favorite class? Who is your favorite teacher?

- Who is your best friend? Why?

- What makes you happiest?

- What magical power would you choose to have?

- How do you see your life in the future?

- Describe yourself in five words or less.

- If you could spend one day doing anything you wanted what would you do?

- What is the best thing about being you?

The goal of asking all these questions is to help you get a firmer grasp on your child's personality. You must know who your child is before you can predict what they are willing to do. Even more importantly, your child must know he or she can come to you. Parent/Agent trust is essential. Your child must trust you enough to know that you won't shut them down when they are being truly honest with you. At the moment your child is his or her most authentic is the moment you have to be the least judgmental. Doing so will make it easier to advise and direct your student. But it all starts with real conversations.

That doesn't mean you and your child will always agree. Remember what I wrote at the beginning of this chapter's segment? Your child is not you. In our household, the parents are outgoing, but the children are not. At first we wanted them to be more like us. But, we had to see each child for who they were. This was not the time to live vicariously through them (although I think all parents want to do that). You must accept and honor their individuality. You can help children make better decisions for their future by doing things like talking to them in a way that elevates them. Look at them, not only as your children, but as a whole person. That's a job for a Parent. You role as Agent is to figure out strategies to help each child be his or her best.

Let me close this section with one more family example. My son and I see life from different points of views. I say, 'up' and he says 'down.' However, I used our different perspectives as an opportunity to help me see who he was so I could give him enough room to have an opinion. This approach also helped establish our roles as Parent/Agent and client/student.

We now have this great grown folks relationship because we got to know each child by letting them speak. Your child doesn't always need to shut up and listen, they actually can express their thoughts about the world around them. This can give insight to their personalities. It's also an example of how to spend time with your child. My son loved video games and he would often ask if I wanted to see him play a video game. I didn't always want to, but guess what?, I did. Those were the moments my son needed. It showed him I cared about the things important to him. If you do the same thing, it will help you represent your child on his or her journey toward getting into college.

Things to do BEFORE High School Classes Start

If you want your child to gain acceptance to the college of his or her choice, you have to start engaging them at a young age. A well thought out college planning process doesn't have to be stressful and it won't be, if it's started years before your student sends out applications. That's not just me speaking. It's the opinion of experts. If possible, parents should introduce their children to the prospect of college in middle school.

If you really have the time to plan, you can start making decisions that will affect your child's college choices while they are in elementary school. Here are some suggestions.

COLLEGE PREPARATION FOR YOUR CHILD IN ELEMENTARY SCHOOL: #1
Talk About Grades and Career Exploration

Every child has the right to dream. If those dreams are fantastical, so what? You should appreciate your child's ability to articulate his or her desires. Don't shoot them down.

COLLEGE PREPARATION FOR YOUR CHILD IN ELEMENTARY SCHOOL: #2
Stop by a Local College Campus for a Sporting Event or Other Activities

If there aren't a lot of successful college graduates in your life, find them. Attend something your child will find fun or interesting. If there isn't a large college nearby, look to the community colleges in your area. The goal is to provide exposure in real life. Get your child away from the computer and video games. Introduce them to real people. The 100 Black Men of America have a slogan that applies, 'What they see is what they'll be.' Show your child a world that includes joy and prosperity any way you can.

COLLEGE PREPARATION FOR YOUR CHILD IN ELEMENTARY SCHOOL: #3
Gradually Introduce the Idea of College by Sharing Your Own Experience or Those of a Relative, Neighbor or Friend

Children like to see success. They specifically like to see successful people who look like them.

COLLEGE PREPARATION FOR YOUR CHILD IN ELEMENTARY SCHOOL: #4

Plant Seeds That Let Them See College as a Possibility in Their Lives

Small children need hope and direction. These are the years of their lives where your level headedness will inspire them, even though they won't understand it. College seems a life-time away to them, and it is. But you know how time flies. Help them see college as an achievable future goal.

COLLEGE PREPARATION FOR YOUR CHILD IN ELEMENTARY SCHOOL: #5

Help Your Children Link the Concept of Success with College

As your child gets older, develops friends and begins to see which subjects or activities he or she likes, you should share how going to college will help them take more control over their lives. The path you started in elementary school should continue in middle school. Here are my suggestions.

COLLEGE PREPARATION FOR YOUR CHILD IN MIDDLE SCHOOL: #1

Increase the Frequency of Conversations about College

COLLEGE PREPARATION FOR YOUR CHILD IN MIDDLE SCHOOL: #2
Talk with Your Child About the Finances Concerning College

Let me elaborate here because it's a very important point.
As you talk to your child about family finances, don't focus on what you can and can't afford,   but instead which options may be viable if he or she gets good grades and receives merit-based aid. (Some money for college is awarded without regard for financial need. This type of college aid is usually awarded for a student's academic achievements in high school, as well as for special talents and unique traits, such as musical or athletic skills.) Begin thinking about scholarship opportunities, some of which are open to high school freshmen.

COLLEGE PREPARATION FOR YOUR CHILD IN MIDDLE SCHOOL: #3
Help Your Child Identify the Qualities of a College that are Good for Them.

Early College Research
While you are helping your child understand the importance of college, you have to spend time on your own finding out what different types of college offer your child. Should they choose to attend a large, public institution? Would your child do better at a

small, private college? Is your child emotionally equipped to live far from home? Will your child flourish at a fiercely competitive university? Does your child have an analytical mind that does well in very structured environment? You have to be able to answer these questions about your child to help them find an institution that uniquely fits him or her.

STEPS THAT WILL HELP YOU CHOOSE THE COLLEGE BEST FOR YOUR CHILD:

1. Consider finances before you determine whether your child will attend school in-state or out-of-state, public or private.

2. Become familiar with types of colleges and universities.

3. Examine types of merit and financial aid a college can offer your child.

4. Keep your geographical options open. Research schools that are close to home and some farther away.

5. Don't let a college sell you on hype. Selective or very expensive schools may not be your child's best education option.

6. Your college bound student should consider his or her own preferences and what they are looking for in a school before making a choice.

There are basic facts you need to know about various types of higher education facilities. More of this information will be described later in the book. But for now, here's a brief review on the difference between public and private institutions, types of colleges and universities, large and small colleges or universities and admission criteria. However, the first topic to tackle is tuition costs.

FUNDING AND TUITION:

Tuition is a fancy word for fees. It is the charge a university or college expects you to pay to allow your children to attend classes. Payments are due before your child enrolls. To learn more about tuition, you first must recognize that private and public institutions are funded by distinctly different means.

PRIVATE vs. PUBLIC INSTITUTIONS:

When it comes to deciding what colleges to apply to, location as well as private vs. public should be a major decision factor. Private schools tend to carry a much higher tuition bill, but the added cost may be worth it if the school is the right fit. The question is how important is that match for that particular school and how much are you able to financially sacrifice? In other words, how much can you really afford?" Don't depend on the opinions of others. Some people are quick to speak on the merits and prestige of private colleges, while others insist they are not worth their tuition bill. My opinion is both types of schools offer their own assets and drawbacks. I created a quick overview to help you understand what they are.

FACTS ABOUT PUBLIC INSTITUTIONS:

1. They are funded primarily through state taxes. Because of that fact, residents who decide to remain in-state for college are able to attend at a lower cost. Your tax dollars have already helped to pay for your child's in-state education. For the same reason, out-of-state tuition is often still lower (on paper) than private school tuition because of taxpayer allocations.

2. On average, public institutions tend be a lot larger than private ones. It's not unusual for the undergraduate populations for public colleges to have more than 20,000 undergraduate students. That's something you have to consider if your child doesn't do well with large setting.

3. Public colleges and universities provide a much wider selection of course offerings, available majors and degrees.

4. Admission priority is typically granted to in-state applicants. However, students at public universities sometimes have trouble enrolling in the classes they need to graduate.

FACTS ABOUT PRIVATE INSTITUTIONS:

1. Private colleges are funded exclusively by tuition, endowments and donations.

2. The cost of attending a private institution of higher learning is more expensive than attending a state-run university or college.

3. Private colleges have fewer major options. However, they are offered in a more concentrated manner.

4. Undergraduate enrollment is often smaller, which usually means smaller class sizes.

5. Private colleges often give students better access to professors.

While the cost of private college might seem exorbitant to many, these schools often offer generous aid packages to undergrads who demonstrate financial need.

However, it's also necessary to mention that the smaller a student population is, the more homogenous it might feel in other ways, such as racial, ethnic or in socioeconomic diversity.

It's important to note that there are definitely exceptions. You can find small public institutions that provide plenty of personal attention and private colleges with a myriad of research opportunities. Indeed, public vs. private isn't about better or worse. When deciding on where to apply, it should really come down to whether or not a school meets your academic, financial and social needs. Remember, a lot of what your child gets out of college depends on what everyone puts into it and that goes for the largest state school or the smallest liberal arts college.

TYPES OF INSTITUTIONS

There are different types of colleges and universities that may be appropriate for your child based on his or her goals, personality, activities, interests, and styles of learning. The type of school can be an important factor in your research.

The Liberal Arts: The courses you take in a liberal arts program are designed to enable you to think deeply and critically about ideas which have influenced our human perceptions of the past, the present, and our future. The focus of this program is not to prepare the student for a specific career, but rather to provide a background of philosophical and theoretical concepts with which to view the world and universe, and to provide a constructive direction for the future.

The Pre-Professional Programs: The first two years in this program are usually designed to allow you to take courses in the liberal arts, but one course per year will be in the area of your career choice. The last two years will enable you to specialize in courses which are designed to prepare you for admission to graduate school, and you are able to concentrate in the courses directly related to that end.

Keep in mind that large universities usually contain more than one type of college. For example, New York University has a College of Arts and Sciences, which offers straight liberal arts programs, and they also have schools with pre-professional programs in business, medicine, performing arts and education.

Institutes of Technology - two year: These schools provide knowledge and practical experience in one specific area (carpentry, secretarial, electronics, agriculture, hotel and restaurant management, etc.). The courses offered are practical in nature, and entirely career-oriented. However, transfer into four year colleges is possible in some programs.

Institutes of Technology - four years: These schools provide knowledge of specific areas in scientific or technical fields, and give you practical experience in laboratory and research projects. Although subjects identified in liberal arts programs are required, their focus is frequently on application to your field of career preparation. Be certain of the field of interest when considering an Institute of Technology.

Specialized Colleges and Schools: The focus is on your talent or concrete career objectives when you attend a specialized college. Musical conservatories, art schools, business schools, automotive schools, and hospital schools of nursing are examples.

As you begin to conduct research about college, continue talking to your children. When we asked ours what they wanted to be when they grew up, we also shared what it would take to turn those dreams into realities. We always had conversations with them, which are paying off now. I'd like to think the time we took to do our part as Parent/Agents during their quest for a college, helped them become successful adults today.

A professional agent doesn't get paid unless his clients land good (and high paying contracts). A good Parent/Agent must make success the standard in your home, though not necessarily tied to finance. I remember asking my children when they knew they wanted to go to college. At the end of this book both of them answer that question in their own words. When you establish a standard of excellence founded on love, and executed as a Parent/Agent, your child knows the next steps and can follow the blueprint that you have laid out.

Of course, none of that matters if the admission requirements are something beyond your child's reach. It is therefore in your best interests to also research admissions criteria so you can get a sense of what's expected, before you pay the fees required to submit an application packet or take the considerable time necessary to fill one out.

FACTS ABOUT ADMISSIONS CRITERIA:

Every college or university has a different set of criteria for admittance. Some require very high GPAs (grade point averages). Others may expect an essay to accompany the student's application packet. There's no way to meet all the standards for all of the schools. For that reason you should visit www.CollegeData.com. This web site allows you to search the college of your choice and click on its name to view its College Profile. You can also find out which colleges accept the Common Application, as well as their application deadlines, fees, and writing requirements. This is vital to the admissions process. You'll learn more about the Common Application in Chapter 7 of this book.

Some of what you should learn about each college or university as you begin your search is listed below. You should know each:

• School's location
• School's population size
• Major your child might want to choose
• System of support developing your child's athletic ability
• Amount of diversity the college's campus life offers
• Tuition, room and board and fees
• Admissions criteria

It's imperative to recognize that you cannot go by sticker price alone for any school. Many institutions offer other incentives to help make them attractive to prospective students. But until you do the necessary research you won't know which school has financial or academic packages that will make your child's journey to college easier.

If your first thought is, 'this is going to take a lot of time,' you're right. It does. That's why I recommend making this a regular part of your weekly schedule. Start tackling this task and begin the search for answers about colleges years before your child can apply. If you try to cram everything you need to know and do into a few short weeks during your child's senior year in high school, something will slip through the cracks. Even worse, the lack of time may force you to make decisions that are potentially disastrous for your college bound child. Your mistakes could hurt his or her chances in life. That's why time management is a make or break it component in your ability to become a successful Parent/Agent.

Developing the Skill of Long-range Time Management

Let's review some of the information you've gained from this book so far. You know that learning your child's strengths is an important part in the college selection process. You know that understanding where you can find tuition money is something you have to research and you know that deadlines can not be ignored. Finally, know that information about the college application process exists, but you don't know about specific college scholarships, what types of recommendations are needed, scholastic aptitude tests or even where the schools your child might want to attend are located.

How do you find all the facts related to those topics? Well, get started early and set up a Google calendar, then stick to any schedule you create. It's time to get organized.

ORGANIZATION: THE KEY TO GOOD TIME MANAGEMENT

A good Parent/Agent knows that he or she will have to keep track of hundreds of documents. If you start the process of finding a good college that fits your child's personality while they are in middle school – it means you will keep track of information for years. Even if you start the gathering process during your child's high school years you'll need multiple sets of facts for a variety of schools.

If you learn how to keep track of everything you need, you'll be ahead of the game. My first suggestion is to create a real and virtual folder for each college you plan to research. Store the documents you need in these folders and focus on researching the items on the list below.

ORGANIZING YOURSELF and YOUR STUDENT: RESEARCH CHECKLIST

College:_____

_____ Public or Private

_____ Location (in-state, out-of-state, miles away from home)

_____ Setting (rural, suburban, urban)

_____ Size – school population

_____ Type of college or university (liberal arts, conservatory, etc.)

_____ Are SAT or ACT required

_____ Are SAT Subject tests required

_____ What is the target GPA

_____ Is an essay required

_____ How many recommendation letters are needed

_____ What is the application deadline

_____ Are there any early application options (early decision and/or early action)

_____ What methods do they accept applications

_____ Tuition costs

_____ Room and board costs

_____ Is a CSS Profile required

_____ Types of merit awards and scholarships available

_____ Are AP and/or IB exams accepted for college credit – if so what scores are accepted

The tasks on this list require diligence to get done properly. You now can see why you have to act as your college bound child's agent while also being a parent. When you review the list, it may seem as if you're doing most of the work at this point. However, your child will need to participate in this process, specifically as he or she gets older. In addition, you need to keep your college bound child engaged.

The best skill your child can develop is a life-long love of learning. Here's why. You can't predict what college courses will lead to solid career choices. Remember, the technology that gave us iPhones and WiFi didn't exist for most of us until after 1999. If you started college that year anything you studied in that field was obsolete by the time you graduated. It's a scary concept, but there is a weapon to protect your child. It's called discovery learning.

Discovery learning is a way of exploring concepts in order to develop new ideas and new models of thinking and behavior. Instead of being given concrete answers, children learn by trying and discarding; they learn through investigating options and discussing possibilities.

TAKE TIME TO DEVELOP DISCOVERY LEARNING SKILLS in YOUR COLLEGE BOUND CHILD

1. Expose your child to new experiences that you think may interest them.

2. Ask them questions and allow them to express themselves freely.

3. Instead of giving them answers ask them what they think of possible solutions.

4. Allow them to experiment with different options.

5. Show them other people who have and successfully use a similar talent.

These tips are in the time management segment for one reason. You have to schedule portions of your week to spend time with your child and make this happen.

Now that you have a research check list, the next question you might ask is when to start applying to colleges or universities.

WHEN DO YOU AND YOUR CHILD START SENDING OUT COMPLETED APPLICATIONS?

The summer before your senior year is the best time to start.

Most students do the majority of their application work in the fall of their senior year. The research checklist in this section will give you a head start. However, you will need a customized list for each college when you begin to apply.

My final list of items for time management is as follows:

- Do as much as you possibly can as soon as you can
- Keep a good schedule that you update regularly and share with your student (Again, Google contacts is a great tool for this)
- Stay ahead of the process, don't let dates sneak up on you
- Don't rush, this is the easiest way to miss or forget something

YOUR COLLEGE BOUND CHILD'S PREPARATION

Most applications ask your college bound child to describe what he or she has done in and out of the classroom. You can't starting thinking about these type of activities the second semester of the child's senior year. As the Agent you have to help your child start thinking about activities, honors and awards years before the information is needed. Now you see why I say preparation for college can start before high school.
Organization and time management counts here also. It's your job as a parent to make a list of those that mean the most to your child. You can also write down some notes on his or her favorite classes and the reasons he or she likes them.

But if you've done the research I've recommended, you already know the types of activities colleges may want to see. You can share that information with your child and both of you can choose activities and organizations that help to develop a well-balanced successful adult. One of the facts you'll have to keep in mind is that at some point your child will have to write about himself or herself. It's another project that will require time.

THE BIG QUESTION

If you do the research and interact with your college bound student and help them schedule activities, there is one question your child will start to ask. Where should I go? You know that several colleges or universities will suit them (because you're a great Parent/Agent!) But your college bound child will have to learn the ins and outs of the selection process for themselves.

At my house, we set the following standard. We told our children that if they did well in school, they could attend any college anywhere. That's because we knew that good grades give a child great options. We also instilled the following idea in our children. We told them that they had to do more than the minimum or try to just get by. A child must position him or herself as best as possible in the eyes of the people accepting college applications. You, the Parent/Agent must help your college bound student to do the best he or she can with the most he or she can handle.

A key part of this process meant incorporating my college bound children into my calendar.

The schedule wasn't rigid, but I would set my expectation in advance to remind them by saying things like, "Thursday we need to set time to go over your application." It was as simple as me telling them what had to be done, how I was going to help and set the expectation of what I needed them to accomplish. I wanted to make sure they understood the importance of doing work on the front end to make it so much easier for them on the back end. That process also applies to finances and is so much easier said, than done.

The Finance Talk

It's important to have a grown-up conversation with your child about college expectations. A frank discussion can help everyone get on the same page. Here are some talking points.

DISCUSSING HOW TO PAY FOR COLLEGE WITH YOUR CHILD

If your child is interested in schools that have significant price differences, you may want to tell them what you can contribute to both options and how you plan to do it. But also let them know what they will have to do as their contribution (job, work study, loans etc.) You can use an online calculator to show your child exactly what it will cost each month over a standard 10-year repayment term. Next, print out an amortization table, showing the breakdown of principal and interest payments that will be due each year.

Be sure you review the basic deferment and forbearance rules that govern the circumstances borrowers can temporarily postpone their federal student loan payments.

Finally, make sure to put that student loan payment into context. There will be many items competing for your child's financial resources after college. Your goal, during this talk, is to help your child understand the long-term financial impact of going to college and to let him or her see the impact of choosing the a more expensive college.

The ideal time to do this is during your child's teenage years. This may be a difficult concept for your teen to fully grasp. But going to college is a serious endeavor and paying for it is no joke. Few children understand everything in one talk and you shouldn't try to give them all you know about college finances all at once. Remember as an excellent Parent/Agent you've been doing research for years.

One final note about college finances.

DON'T BAIT-AND-SWITCH

If you spend years telling a child that he or she can go to college, don't renege. I can tell you once again, from experience, that life gets in the way. The closer college costs come to becoming a reality the larger the tuition bill seems. I can also tell you that there is no good time to start saving for your child's education. Do it sooner rather than later, anyway. If you don't you'll find something worse. You'll find out that tuition is due, you've saved nothing and now it's time to seek out loans.

Chapter Two

What Your College Bound Student Should Expect a Parent/Agent to Do

● ●

This chapter will help you set expectations:

▶ The Team and who is Assigned What Positions/Tasks

▶ Time and How Much Should be Allocated to Planning

▶ Who is Responsible for the Execution of Individual Ideas?

▶ Interpersonal Skill Development

▶ Trust

● ●

AGENT POV:

The better your college bound student is positioned, the more chances they have to succeed.

PARENT POV:

The journey to college starts when school starts.

Coming together is a beginning. Keeping together is progress. Working together is success."

~Henry Ford

*I*f you've read the information in the previous chapter you've figured out something. The search for a college is actually a partnership between you and your child. Admittedly, your part starts long before your child realizes that there is a plan in place. But you don't attend classes or earn grades. You don't have to figure out who you are going to be. This is a team effort, but in the beginning, only the Parent/Agent knows that.

The Team and who is Assigned What Positions/ Tasks

I was the one that had to do the research and my children had to be the ones who went to school. It was a team process and we were ready to lead the charge. If you're going to be a great Parent/Agent you must be able to find abundant options for your client, the college bound student, even down to the summer camps. This was very important because you probably feel the same way my husband and I do when it comes to our kids.

They're the most important part of us, the best gift that we could have ever received. We as parents help them develop, build character, implement great study habits, find their passion, identify opportunities for them to grow, expose them to things that will help them learn and position them for success.

Doing all these things is where the team aspect develops. We as Parent/Agents are responsible for seeing that our children get the best deals possible in their lives. But it's our children who have to go to these activities. They have to participate. That makes this a team process. Sometimes, a good Parent/Agent has to find opportunities that will open doors that help them learn to become successful on their own.

The ultimate goal for me as the Parent/Agent for my children, was to get them to a college or university that would help them become the adults that I envisioned. But, I also wanted them to do well in life. Their success was my reward. For me, it's not monetary, but rather the reward of seeing them happy, thriving, healthy and doing something they love. However, I knew I had my job cut out for me.

Here's what I had to do as a developing Parent/Agent:
- Determine if my children were serious and willing to do the work to improve
- Push them to prove themselves
- Get them involved in extracurricular activities
- Seek out opportunities that fit their personalities
- Not waste money if it didn't make sense

Here's what I know as an educator. When kids are forced they often don't finish and everyone loses. Both money and time go down the drain. You must know your children are ready and that college is right for them. They must have their mindset right and know where they fit and have a perspective of what they could be or all your efforts are wasted if they aren't ready.

Once you have a willing participant you have to add other members to your team. You must also develop a support team to help you navigate through this maze of information. Don't procrastinate, just get it done. Sure you can do it alone, but why? There other parents going through the same thing you are. There also may be parents that have already completed the path you just started. They can be a wealth of knowledge. A group of mothers I knew began an online group to share information and resources. They were part of each other's team.

This was a great way to help share information, make sure everyone was on task and had the access to the tools to make the process as simple as possible. You must also enlist those that have the skillset you need or maybe even something as simple as time. They may support you by picking your child up from practice if you're running late.

The village concept is an important aspect of the college preparation process. When you have a team of individuals that have a common goal, you all work more on purpose to ensure individuals and ultimately group success.

Listen to your support team. Get objective opinions about your child's abilities. Not only will you get unbiased feedback, you will have their support. Also, do your best to see the process through your children's eyes. This will remind you that the most important contribution you can make is to help the kids be conscious of the journey and use the process to grow.

Time and How Much Should be Allocated to Planning

There is no magic formula for what you want to accomplish. However, I do want to give you some guidelines that will help you build a schedule that will work for you and your family. Let me start by asking you to tap into a few memories. Remember when your child was very small? Remember the time it took to feed, change diapers, get them to sleep and generally watch over them almost 24 hours a day?

Well, the good news is now there are no diapers involved and you won't start out needing a schedule that will consume most of your day. However, you do have to carve how significant chunks of time. You might want to start with something like devoting the equivalent of an entire afternoon to them during their elementary and middle school years. This doesn't mean the time you spend with them during a regular week. Add time to take them places that will help them see a future for themselves that includes college.

The other factor about budgeting for time is that what you start will increase as your children get older.

During high school you need to dedicate more time to planning for your child's college search. This does not include the time you will use for vacations planned to visit college campuses, phone calls, college fairs and interaction with high school counselors.

This book will provide you with detailed lists, contacts, web sites and personal examples of what has worked in my family. Allocating the right amount of time over a really long period of time is a key component to accomplishing the goals you want to achieve for your child. There are no shortcuts. Once you accept this, you have taken a major step toward becoming an outstanding Parent/Agent for your college bound student.

Who is Responsible for the Execution of Individual Ideas?

You have to help your child make informed decisions about his or her education. It is your job as the Parent/Agent to set goals that align with the vision. Again, an example from my family may help you. Our son wants to be a motion picture director and saw himself putting a film together. This was his thing and he was always focused on what he wanted to do. Someone described an editing job and the Parent/Agent in me could see the match. By knowing him, I knew this could be a perfect career fit and today he currently works for a major editing company. College for him was a stepping stone toward his path of choice. He had a vision and college was going to help him make it a reality.

Here are some keys that may help your student get into a college that will help him or her have the same outcome:

1. Get an early start and finish strong: Colleges want to see that you've focused from the start on getting the best possible education your high school has to offer.

2. Challenge them responsibly: While grades remain the single biggest factor in admissions decisions, strength of curriculum is very important as well to show a degree of challenge.

3. There's room for error, with an explanation: You don't need a perfect record to get into the school of your dreams. You must, however, provide an explanation for any significant blip.

Of course, there are the basics you have to cover in your role as a Parent/Agent. Your children must:

1. do well academically
2. be active in clubs and organizations
3. participate in extracurricular activities in and out of school
4. learn about colleges
5. find the best possible opportunities for a college education.

4. Don't just join: Top colleges are increasingly after well-rounded student bodies of individual specialists: the football player, the poet, the mathematician. So it's better to be involved in fewer activities wholeheartedly over time, rather than 9 or 10 half way.

Of course, there are the basics you have to cover in your role as a Parent/Agent. Your children must:

1. do well academically

2. be active in clubs and organizations

3. participate in extracurricular activities in and out of school

4. learn about colleges

5. find the best possible opportunities for a college education.

What do you want to be when you grow up? This question always plants seeds for thought. As a Parent/Agent you have to see your child's future and envision them as adults. If you plan correctly you start to see them that way long before they can do it themselves.

By the time they share the vision with you the reality of being grown up is right at their doorsteps. My daughter is a strong writer, so journalism seemed to be a good fit for her. But the Parent/Agent in me kept looking for other aspects of the business. When Oprah did a behind the scenes segment that introduced producers I knew immediately that was a job my child could do. In fact, that's one of her career aspirations. Did I know any television producers? No, but I did know my child. The goal was to find a worthwhile goal that would fit her talents.

While professional agents benefit financially by receiving a percentage of the contract they help their clients secure, parent agents on the other hand receive the reward of their children matriculating through college successfully and get the job of their dreams to begin their adult lives. Becoming a great Parent/Agent for your teen is often a matter of having a few key qualities, both in terms of personality traits and skill set.

Successful Parent/Agents tend to be problem solvers. They are great at analyzing options and making strong decisions. When looking at the details of a college, you should have the ability to quickly determine if it's a good fit for your child and identify the most beneficial solutions possible.

Parent/Agents are often positioned between the aspirations of the student and the college/university of interest to them. A great Parent/Agent knows how to communicate effectively and concisely, to convey necessary information. Multitasking is also key quality as parent agent. Whether it's simultaneously juggling responsibilities at home, your "other" full time job, multiple children, keeping track of dates, extracurricular activities, college visits, fairs and other events to top position your client/child. Along with multitasking comes strong organizational skills and the ability to manage, not only your time well, but show your client/child how to manage his or her time well also.

Interpersonal Skill Development

You must show your teens how to build relationships with the key individuals that can help them on this journey such as their high school counselor, teachers, club/organization leaders and college representatives from the schools they're interested in attending. Great Parent/Agents are able to work together with their clients/students to find options that work well for all parties involved.

You and your college bound student must walk hand-in-hand with trust. This is the quality of honesty. Be forthright and truthful, it is also important that a parent agent not just tell their child what they want to hear. If they are truly not Ivy League material you must be honest and point them in the right direction, rather than waste time and resources pursuing options that could never happen. It is up to you to help them understand and get excited about the possible places that could be a good fit for them based on their abilities, skill set and career goals. It's important to help showcase your child's academic ability and pair them with the opportunities that will help them become the best they can be.

The process can be long and confusing, but the more you know as a Parent/Agent, the easier it will be to get that coveted acceptance letter and the potential scholarships to boot. You must be confident as you serve as their guide. Help identify the best schools, prepare for required entrance exams, seek funding and prepare them for college and the life they will live beyond it.

Trust

By building trusting relationships you create an honest environment to encourage them. Helping your child to develop self-awareness is a critical piece of this puzzle. If you haven't already, this is a great time to discuss the importance of being able to trust one another because you have their best interests at heart. Ultimately, you want your kids to be engaged in this process and committed to doing their part, which mainly should be being the best student they can be to increase all of their options.

Encouraging your child to love learning makes a difference in this process as it expands their ability to open doors. Students who love to learn generally get much better grades. A passion for learning is quite different from just studying to earn a grade or to please parents and teachers. Those who develop a love of learning at an early age continue the process throughout their lives and are generally more successful, interesting, and happier than those who don't.

You can engage your kids to promote the love of learning by seeing how they feel about various issues (current events, relationships, values). Allow them to have opinions without passing judgment. Ask your children to help you understand why they feel the way they do. It doesn't take much effort to inspire a child's brain in the everyday world. After all, it's the world they will live in as adults and the place where they will need an inspired brain the most.

Chapter Three

The High School Timetable

● ●

This chapter breaks down the high school timeline:

▶ 9th Grade

▶ 10th Grade

▶ 11th Grade

▶ 12th Grade

● ●

AGENT POV:

Students must utilize his or her school counselor and build a solid rapport.

PARENT POV:

Once your child is accepted make sure they don't slack off for their senior year. The school of their choice is still looking.

"This time, like all times, is a very good one, if we but know what to do with it."

~Ralph Waldo Emerson

*R*epeat after me, "High School will be easy!" It's all about perspective. This is the step that will set the tone for the rest of your student's life. High schools are places that are vital to help our children get ready to function in the adult world. High School not only gives them the lessons in the form of classes, but it helps them get the experience they need through everyday skills too. High school is the proving ground for college. It's the opportunity for your child to show that they are college material. They have to understand there's a blueprint for success, that if followed can position them to have the life they want. The thing to remember here is that many of our children may not know exactly what they want out of life just yet. It's our role as Parent/Agents to guide them and help them to make the right decisions. It's important to not cross over to the point where you do it all for them, as that would be doing them a huge disservice. They have to buy-in to see that you have a vision even if they don't actually see it themselves. Understand when you have to step in and do it for them, but know when to say when.

High school can be a very challenging time for young people. It's those critical four years before entering college. It's also a time when kids are becoming young adults, learning about friendships and relationships, and coming into their own personalities by discovering who they are. They're learning somewhat more advanced material, and they are preparing themselves to go out into the real world. Do your best to remember this and help them to make the smoothest transition possible.

You must focus on variables that you do have control over. You must ask yourself:
1. What do you want to transpire at the end of this process?
2. What are you willing to sacrifice to make it a reality?
3. What are you going to do to move forward?
4. How will you capitalize on a rare opportunity for your student?

To do that you need a four-year plan.

You may want to start as early as the end of the student's eighth-grade year to get ahead of the curve. You need to proactively make the most of your student's high school career. Since this is a team process, your children must have some ownership in it. This will help teach them responsibility. By working together as a team, you have their back as they forget deadlines and procrastinate to get some things done.

Being solution oriented means that you are an effective problem solver. The problem you're solving here is your child has not been accepted to the college of his or her choice, and maybe they haven't identified the right college for them yet. These are problems that you can solve.

You must let your children develop the independence and responsibilities instrumental to their development in different ways. However, some of the things that need to be done are too important to use as a teaching tool. It will be up to you to switch those parent and agent hats back and forth. Have your child sit with you so he or she can stay informed and understand the process. You, Ms. or Mr. Parent/Agent represent them, and must be armed with the resources to maximize their high school career.

Students spend a lot of time and money just preparing for college admissions. Fall seems to always be right around the corner, which means it's always time for colleges across the country to prepare to welcome incoming students from around the world. It also means it's time for those high school students that live in your house and who have intentions of pursuing higher education to get prepared. Similar to an athlete who has their hopes set on going to the pros would prepare to be drafted.

Think of it this way. High school is the proving ground for the pros. A lot of the decisions you need to make about college start by understanding what is needed. I've provided several checklists with support timetables to help you.

Pre-High School Checklist:
FOR COLLEGE BOUND STUDENT

_____ Start thinking about which high school classes will best prepare you for college.

_____ Take challenging classes in English, mathematics, science, history, geography, the arts, and a foreign language.

_____ Develop strong study skills (SEE RESOURCES AT BOOK'S END).

_____ If you have an opportunity to choose among high school or can select different programs within one high school, investigate the options and determine which ones will help you further your academic and career interests and open doors to many future options.

_____ Find a mentor who will support your positive goals and help you with questions about plans for your future.

_____ This is also a good time to start researching summer options. Colleges offer enrichment programs and summer opportunities based on student's interest. Go to a college's website and search for summer opportunities for high school students.

Your town, city and state also have opportunities for you to take advantage of. For our children, we researched this information. As a result, both of them secured an internship through an application process for our town.

Our son was involved in the NAACP ACT-SO Program and attended a pre-college program in the summer. Our daughter's high school connected her with a local newspaper that allowed her to participate in a year long internship. One summer, she was selected for a competitive summer journalism program. In addition they volunteered and were active in either sports or clubs. The summers especially is a great time to take advantage of enriching opportunities and programs.

Timetable For 9th Grade: The High School Freshman's Year

Ninth grade is typically the year every grade counts, the year of the permanent record. Despite the challenges, most kids and their parents manage to make the transition from middle to high school with minimal challenges. It's important to learn good organizational skills so you and your child can live a balanced life, with time for schoolwork, friends, family, and activities.

9th grade checklist: FOR COLLEGE BOUND STUDENT

_____ Build strong academic skills by taking challenging courses

_____ Study hard and get excellent grades

_____ Become involved in school activities

_____ Volunteer for community activities

_____ Meet with your counselor to discuss your plans for the next four years

_____ Ask your counselor for a list of core courses required

_____ Find out NCAA (National Collegiate Athletic Association) requirements if you want to play sports in college

_____ Begin building your student resume by keeping track of your activities, honors, work experience and academic record

9th Grade Checklist: FOR PARENT/AGENT OF COLLEGE BOUND STUDENT

_____ Monitor that challenging classes are taken in English, mathematics, science, history, geography, a foreign language, government, civics, economics and the arts

_____ Get to know the school's career counselor or school counselor

_____ Find other college resources available in your child's school

_____ Have your child talk to adults in a variety of professions to determine what he or she likes and dislikes about different jobs and what kind of education is needed for each kind of career

9th Grade Checklist: FOR PARENT/AGENT and STUDENT/CLIENT

_____ Explore career options by using search tools

_____ Register for SAT subject tests, if appropriate

_____ Continue saving money for college

Timetable for 10th Grade: The High School Sophomore's Year

The classes your child takes in grade 10 will determine the courses they qualify to take in grades 11 and 12. Find out what you need to know about college prep in the 10th grade. This is also the year when more of the actual performance load shifts to the student. Here's a suggested check list for them.

10th Grade Checklist: FOR COLLEGE BOUND STUDENT

_____ Continue building a strong academic record

_____ Continue to participate in activities and community service

_____ Consult with your school counselor about taking the PSAT as a sophomore

_____ Attend College Fairs – check with your local counselor, associations or your high school

_____ Review PSAT results with your counselor

_____ Take challenging courses in English, mathematics, science, history, geography, a foreign language, government, civics, economics, and the arts

_____ Continue to talk to adults in a variety of professions to determine what they like and dislike about their jobs, and what kind of education is needed for each kind of job

_____ Speak with your teachers and counselor about challenging yourself with Honors and/or AP course(s)

_____ Participate in school or community-based extracurricular activities that interest you and enable you to explore career interests

_____ Meet with your career counselor or school counselor to discuss colleges and their requirements

_____ Take advantage of opportunities to visit colleges and talk to college students

10th grade checklist: FOR PARENT/AGENT OF COLLEGE BOUND STUDENT

You don't have a checklist. But that doesn't mean you get to take a break. Everything is about to ramp up. You need to start making plans to visit colleges with your student. It is your job to subtly monitor his or her activities and make sure they will make good essay or extracurricular demonstrations of balance on college application forms. If you haven't started saving – check tuition costs and put it in gear.

Timetable for 11th Grade: The High School Junior's Year

Eleventh grade is a key year in the college planning process, with standardized test taking, narrowing your college list, and investigating financial aid. Find out more about college prep in your junior year of high school. Eleventh grade is the perfect time to visit colleges during your child's spring break.

JUNIOR YEAR

August - September

- Get off to a strong start in school

- Register/take PSAT (more than likely given at your school)

- Continue to research colleges to visit and apply to

- If planning to play a sport at a DI or DII college, check with counselor to make sure you are on track with all of the NCAA core courses

- Continue to participate in school and community activities

October - January

- Begin to research/develop a preliminary college list – use college reference books, the Internet and speak to graduates you know attending college

- Register for SAT, SAT subject and/or ACT tests

- Make sure you are on track to meet your graduation requirements

- PSAT results available

February - March

- Continue to surf the Web for college, career, and scholarship information

- Begin visiting colleges you have interest in (spring break is an excellent time to see colleges)

- Call college admissions office for information on college tours and informational sessions

- Select courses for senior year that are both challenging and appropriate for your future goals

- Research summer opportunities – pre-college, enrichment and internship programs

April - June

- Take appropriate SAT/ACT test

- Attend college fairs – check with your local counselor associations or your high school

- Organize your filing system for college materials

- Make appointments for tours and/or interviews and visit colleges

- Take your AP tests

- Request teacher recommendation letters

- Finalize your resume of activities

- Send SAT or ACT scores to NCAA Eligibility Center if you are playing a sport in college and register if you have not already done so at eligibilitycenter.org

July - August

- Use summer vacations wisely, i.e. continue visiting colleges, (call college admissions office for info on college visits and informational sessions), take courses for enrichment, do volunteer work/community service, get a job, etc.

- Begin organizing possible essays for colleges

- Create a concrete list of colleges you are applying to

NOTES for JUNIORS

- AP testing is in May

- National, local and school college fairs – usually fall and spring – useful info on the NACAC (National Association for College Admission Counseling) website about national fairs in your area http://www.nacacnet.org/studentinfo/Pages/Default.aspx

- College testing

  - ACT – 11th grade Feb., April, and June - 12th grade Sept., Oct. and Dec.

  - SAT – 11th grade Jan., March, May and June - 12th grade Oct., Nov. and Dec.

- Plan to work on your weak areas to help for the SAT and/or ACT taken in your junior year – use khanacademy.com

- Speak with your teachers and counselor about challenging yourself with Honors and/or AP course(s)

- Register with the NCAA Eligibility Center at eligibilitycerter.org (If you want to play a sport in college)

- Explore online resources about colleges, careers, and scholarships available

- Continue doing research

- Register for SAT subject tests, if appropriate

- Continue career exploration by selecting electives within your field of interest

- Update your student resume

- Explore summer enrichment programs offered at universities and local organizations

11th Grade Checklist: FOR COLLEGE BOUND STUDENT

_____ Meet with your career counselor or guidance counselor to discuss colleges and their requirements

_____ Continue involvement in school or community-based extracurricular activities

_____ Decide which colleges most interest you (write these schools to request information and an application for admission, be sure to ask about special admissions requirements, financial aid, and deadlines)

_____ Talk to college representatives at college fairs

_____ Take advantage of opportunities to visit colleges and talk to students

_____ Consider people to ask for recommendations - teachers, counselors, employers, etc.

11th Grade Checklist: PARENT/AGENT OF COLLEGE BOUND STUDENT

_____ Investigate the availability of financial aid from federal, state, local, and private sources

_____ Call the Student Aid Hotline at the U.S. Department of Education (1-800-4FED-AID) for a student guide to Federal financial aid. Talk to your school counselor for more information

CHECKLIST FOR PARENT/AGENT and STUDENT/ CLIENT

_____ Investigate the availability of scholarships provided by organizations such as corporations, labor unions, professional associations, religious organizations, and credit unions.

_____ If applicable, go online and search for directories of scholarships for women, minorities, and disabled students.

_____ Register for and take the SAT, ACT, SAT Subject Tests, or any other exams required for admission to colleges you might want to attend. If you have difficulty paying the registration fee, see your school counselor about getting a fee waiver.

Timetable for 12th Grade: The High School Senior's Year

Early fall for 12th grade students is a great time to visit colleges Once your child reaches senior year, the college search kicks up a notch and will sometimes feel like a full-time job. Find out more about college prep in the 12th grade.

STUDENT SENIOR YEAR CHECKLIST

_____ Take challenging classes in English, mathematics, science, history, geography, a foreign language, government, civics, economics, the arts, and advanced technologies

_____ Meet with your counselor early in the year to discuss your plans

_____ Complete all necessary financial aid forms

_____ Email colleges to request information and applications for admission. Be sure to ask about financial aid, admissions requirements, and deadlines

_____ If possible, visit the colleges that most interest you

_____ Register for and take the SAT, ACT, SAT Subject Tests, or any other exams required for admission to the colleges to which you are applying

_____ Prepare your application carefully (Follow the instructions, and pay close attention to deadlines!)

_____ Be sure to ask your counselor and teachers at least two weeks before your application deadlines to submit the necessary documents to colleges (your transcript, letters of recommendation, etc.)

August - September

- If you intend to play a sport at a Division I or II college, make sure you are on track for all of your core courses

- Register for the SAT, SAT Subject Tests and ACT fall exams

- Approach teachers for letters of recommendation

- Talk to your counselor about your list of colleges

- Explore scholarship opportunities for colleges you are applying to and research online

- Review your transcript – make sure it is correct

- Attend regional college fairs, high school sponsored fairs and individual admission rep visits if offered at your school

- Apply to colleges – applications are mostly online and you can get applications at the college or at college fairs. Common Application is a popular method of submitting applications.

- Let your school know what colleges you have applied to, so they can send all the supporting documents: transcript, letters of recommendation, etc.

- If you are considering early decision/action, begin obtaining and reading applications thoroughly and inform counselor

October

- Follow up with teachers on college recommendations

- Schedule final college interviews where needed

- Make final college visits, stay overnight at your top choices

- Begin submitting applications; early decision/early action and rolling admissions schools should be submitted first

- Take SAT and/or ACT if needed

- Arrange for all SAT and ACT scores to be sent from the test company to the colleges you are applying to (some high schools may include on your transcript – check with school for their specific process)

- Attend regional college fairs

November

- File CSS profile if applying to private schools – check college to see if needed

- Submit applications with January 1 or 15 deadline dates to let your high school know to avoid the holiday crunch (check with your school for specific deadlines)

- Take SAT if still needed

December

- Finish submitting applications (February due date or later)

- Confirm with colleges that they have received all your test scores and application

- Keep your grades up; mid-year grades may be sent to colleges if required

- Send updated SAT or ACT scores to NCAA Eligibility Center if you are playing a sport in college

January

- Fill out FAFSA online after January 1, but before February 1 (Starting with the class of 2017, the FAFSA can be completed as early as October of their senior year).

February - March

- Mid-year grades may be needed to be mailed to colleges

- File all appropriate forms as soon as possible

- Any applications still not submitted should be completed as soon as possible if the deadline allows

- Notify your counselor of all college acceptances, rejections, and wait-listed status

- Continue to check for scholarships

April - June

- Make final decisions about college. Submit necessary deposit (May 1 is the universal deadline for college deposits)

- Take AP exams (in mid-July have scores sent to college you are attending)

- Report all college decisions to your counselor. Notify him/her about which college you will attend

- Meet all graduation requirements

- Meet all college deadlines to ensure your place in the college of your choice

Certain times of the year are key every year:

- Course scheduling for the next school year

- Summer use as opportunity for enrichment and college visits

- Early Fall for 12th grade students is a great time to visit colleges

- For 11th grade the perfect time to visit colleges is during spring break

- AP testing is in May

- National, local and school College fairs – usually fall and spring – useful info on the NACAC (National Association for College Admission Counseling) website about national fairs in your area http://www.nacacnet.org/studentinfo/Pages/ Default.aspx

College testing

- ACT – 11th grade Feb., April, and June - 12th grade Sept., Oct. and Dec.

- SAT – 11th grade Jan., March, May and June - 12th grade Oct., Nov. and Dec.

- Registration deadlines are usually a month and a half before exam. However, the earlier you register the more likelihood you will get your first choice in testing center.

- SAT Subject Test May or June at the end of the course in the subject area you are taking the test on

Whew! If you think this is a whirlwind of constant work, you're right. Now you see why your student has to take ownership of this process. He or she does almost all of the work during the last two years of high school. But if there is a lifelong love of learning established, these challenges can be met. More than that, they can be conquered.

If all of this looks overwhelming, take a breath and a step back. It can be done and done well. You just have to have faith in yourself and your teen.

Verdel A. Jones

Chapter Four

How to Screen a School to Get the Best Education for Your Child

● ●

This chapter explains the different types of screening options:

▶ Online screening
▶ College Websites
▶ Facebook Pages
▶ Twitter
▶ Pinterest
▶ Instagram
▶ Relationships with Counselors
▶ Contacting Local Alums
▶ College Fairs
▶ The List
▶ The Visit
▶ Financial Aid
▶ The Talk: Part II

● ●

AGENT POV:

Exposure is a key component to getting recognized. Make sure the colleges that you are interested in know your student's name.

PARENT POV:

Once your child is accepted make sure they don't slack off for their senior year. The school of their choice is still looking.

"By failing to prepare, you are preparing to fail."

~ Benjamin Franklin

I've wanted to write this book for years, but actually started putting it together in 2014. One of the topics I have to address as a Parent/Agent is the information age overload. It affects everybody. The amount of information available can be simultaneously exciting and confusing for your college bound child. You want to see them grow into responsible adults who are   prepared to become the next generation of parents, workers, business owners, activists and leaders. Each child needs help getting there.   Every student needs support, guidance, and opportunities during this time. This is a time of rapid growth and change. Your teens will face unique and diverse challenges, both personally and developmentally. All of these changes impact academic achievement.

It's your role as a Parent/Agent to help your college bound child navigate the courses, maximize the opportunities and find the best strategies to make high school years count. The most efficient way to do that is to get digitally connected. Here are some suggestions on how it will help to narrow the list of which colleges are right for your child.

Every school has a website. Most likely the school's website is their name.edu (example: www.towson.edu, www.harvard.edu, www.molloy.edu, etc.). But there are also general websites that can help you get started.

GENERAL WEB SITES THAT CAN AID YOUR SEARCH:
1. Collegeboard.org
2. Petersons.com
3. Collegeview.com

Online Screening

Searching for and applying to colleges is a stressful process. The efficient Parent/Agent and their client/student will find decisions easier to make if they have current and thorough information about the colleges they are considering or ones they may not have considered just yet.

The college search process can sometimes feel overwhelming. There are many different resources that go into developing a balanced college list, but sometimes the tools that are overlooked are the ones many high school students use every day: social media networks. An increasing number of students are utilizing social media to size up prospective schools when developing a balanced college list. While some college admissions representatives use social media to check on applicants, you and your student can also find good unfiltered information about colleges to help you make an informed decision.

1. Search to get an idea of the schools' culture
2. Ask about overnight visits to spend the night in the dorm before application
3. Use hashtags (example #StateCollege, #MyChoiceU)

Google colleges based on the names you know and begin keeping a file.

1. Make categories based on the criteria you are searching such as cost, location, reputation, programs etc.
2. Contact your contacts
3. Review the brochures you have collected and the notes you have taken
4. Make a list of three to five universities where your child can imagine himself or herself as a successful student. (See suggestion for college web surfing below.)
5. As high school teens, students should take the lead in discovering what special talents they have, what they are looking for in a college experience and how they best think and learn.
6. Public vs private institutions (Chapter 1)
7. Don't forget to research two-year vs four year institutions
8. Examine single-sex vs co-ed
9. Discuss campus size: large, medium or small
10. Use a map to pinpoint the campus location: urban, suburban, rural, out of state, in state or international
11. Check the academic offerings
12. Majors
13. Faculty, their experience and degree of education especially in desired field

14. Residential and social life
15. Student organizations and activities
16. Athletics and recreational sports (varsity, intramural and club)
17. Community service organizations
18. Personal and career counseling
19. Extracurricular activities
20. Personal attention available
21. The diversity of student body
22. Religious affiliation

Yes, that's quite a list. It's the reason you have to start on it early in your college bound child's academic career. It's the reason you need separate folders as described in this book's first chapter. It becomes exponentially more difficult as you expand your list of schools.

But wait. There's more. You and your teen now need to work as a team to cover the next set of topics.

QUESTIONS YOUR TEEN HAS TO ANSWER (or ACTIONS HE/SHE MUST TAKE)

1. Determine if they offer majors I enjoy.
2. Email the representatives at the universities on your list to introduce yourself and attend any college fair in your area.
3. If your parents have questions, see if the representative can call or email them.

When you follow up, as a prospective student, you let recruiters know your level of interest. It will be their job to help you with the next steps.

Facebook Pages

An effective social media platform to use during your college search is Facebook. While it's beneficial to "like" Facebook pages and "follow" the Twitter accounts of schools to show demonstrated interest, you and your student can take it a step further by using the information on these networks to build a bigger profile that organizes what you like about a particular institution.

1. For those students who are unable to visit a college in person, virtual tours are sometimes available on a school's website. But often those online guides are not updated regularly, and can leave much to the imagination as to what campus life is actually like.

2. However, on Facebook many schools post current photos and videos that give followers a glimpse into student life on campus.

Twitter

Twitter is a great way to keep track of what's going on at the schools you're interested in applying to. Because of the short-form content and constant updates, prospective students can get a better sense of the news, events, issues, and interactions that happen day-to-day at a particular institution.

1. Many departments within colleges manage their own separate Twitter accounts, so you can get the latest updates on what's going on in a major or course of study you're interested in.

2. Social media managers are often very responsive to questions and comments from followers, so it's a great way to engage in a conversation about aspects that interest you.

3. You can also follow certain "hashtags" that may be associated with a college or university to see what others on Twitter have to say about the school. Some schools and admissions offices even host and participate in Twitter chats with prospective applicants.

4. Follow reporters, counselors, and other experts who can keep you informed on what's going on in the admissions world,

Pinterest

Another social media outlet is Pinterest. It is an excellent research tool to find colleges and universities.

1. You may find a collection of both visual and informational links that can give prospective students a glimpse into the lighter side of the campus culture.

2. Content offered on schools' Pinterest boards is often a mix of campus resources, links to school information and publications, admissions tips, and general information for high school students making the transition into college.

Instagram

We've talked a lot about how visual elements are great ways to get a sense of a campus, and while nothing beats an in-person campus visit, Instagram is another way to get a bigger picture of a college or university. Instagram can give followers a "behind-the-scenes" look at daily life on campus that they might not normally see.

1. Admissions offices have provided "insider photos."

2. Some give first-glimpse images of decision letters ready to go out or the process of preparing for an information session.

Relationships with counselors and coaches

The relationship I had established with the high school counselor at my children's school really helped when I had to ignore my own rules and ditch my timetable for a few months. Our family, like most, had challenges. To minimize them, I contacted the

A COUNSELOR'S RESPONSIBILITY TO YOUR CHILD'S QUEST FOR A COLLEGE

1. They write recommendations

2. They know how to find and have scholarships

3. They administer special programs

4. They can find information for all of the above

counselor and made a request for help. Because we had already established this relationship and the counselor was a part of our team, it was simple. This is the final plank of building your team.

I write this personal story to show how the school counselor is a key component to your child's college aspirations. Many people don't realize this. If the school counselors don't know your children they can't recommend them. It's your job to make sure that introductions happen. High school counselors have a wicked large caseload but they're an important part of the educational leadership team. Counselors provide valuable assistance to students regardless of whether they work in an elementary school or middle school, high school or beyond. Parent/Agents be proactive. Counselors need to be a part of your family's team. You need to ensure that the partnership is made with them.

Now that you know a counselor's importance. Let me say some are overwhelmed with the numbers of students that come to them. So here is a short list of the types of support each counselor should provide to you and your student.

A COUNSELOR'S RESPONSIBILITY TO YOUR CHILD'S QUEST FOR A COLLEGE

1. They write recommendations
2. They know how to find and have scholarships
3. They administer special programs
4. They can find information for all of the above

The high school counselor is a power broker so one of the tasks you have to accomplish as a Parent/Agent is to have your child meet the counselor and introduce themselves. As outlined earlier, sooner is much better than later. It's also easier if your child makes this introduction as a freshman or sophomore instead of a frantic, second semester senior.

Your child can make a huge impression on the counselor by simply scheduling an appointment and asking intelligent questions. You want to make sure that not only do your children know the counselor, but that the counselor knows them. Counselors deal with large numbers of students at the same time so it's imperative that they make the connection to ensure that the counselor knows who they are to be able to plug them into resources and opportunities. The counselor serves as the conduit or connection to help your child get noticed and stay plugged in.

If your child is shy or not a natural conversationalist, here are some suggested questions. Some of them will apply to you.

TEN QUESTIONS YOU and YOUR CHILD SHOULD ASK A HIGH SCHOOL COUNSELOR

1. When is scheduling of classes for the following year? (9th, 10th, or 11th grader)

2. When should my child take college entrance exams? (Agent/Parent)

3. When are deadlines for college entrance exams? (9th, 10th, or 11th grader)

4. Do you have college fairs? When? (9th, 10th, or 11th grader)

5. Do you have college individual visits? When? How do we sign up? (Agent/Parent client/student)

6. What time of year do we meet with you about college? (Agent/Parent client/student)

7. What grade level do you meet with formally to discuss college? (9th grader)

8. What is a resource my child and I use to complete college searches and research? (Agent/Parent client/student)

9. Do you use Naviance? (most schools use this software program).

10. If not, what do you use? (Agent/Parent)

Let me add a final line about another possible resource for your child, coaches. Like the counselor, coaches have a list of information that they can share with deserving students. They can locate scholarships and are a good source for recommendations. If your child is athletically gifted, please reach out to sports coaches the same way you have with the high school counselor.

Contact Local Alums

There are groups that represent almost every college in the country where alums get together. Find them and talk to recent graduates. If you live in an area where that is difficult, email the college and ask about graduates who live close to you.

1. Try to find recent graduates. Someone who earned a degree 20 years ago may not have relevant information

2. Also try to talk to students who have received degrees in the fields your student likes

A note about friends and families with children who also want to attend college. Compare notes with other Parent/Agents, but keep it on a casual and friendly level. The admissions process can too easily begin to feel like a competition. Force yourself to take a break for a bit. Steer conversations away from college talk.

College Fairs

College fairs are one of the most important tools you can use in making a final decision about what college your student wants to apply to. College fairs allow you and your college bound student to get some insight into what a college or university will be like. Parents and students participating in college fairs meet one-on-one with representatives from colleges and universities to discuss admission and financial aid opportunities at their respective institutions. Speaking with the college representatives gives you insight into the heart of the institution. It also gives your student a name, face and hopefully an email to use to get direct answers for direct questions.

Once you locate the fairs, you should register in advance to make the most of your time onsite and ensure that colleges can follow up with you. Please refer to the notes you took on time management.

College fairs present many advantages for students. This opportunity to meet representatives from a range of institutions can be invaluable. It is important that you keep in mind that colleges are big businesses, and there is more than a little competition. As a result, you should expect that college and university representatives are most definitely put there to impress you.

BEFORE YOU AND/OR YOUR CHILD ATTEND A COLLEGE FAIR: DO YOUR RESEARCH

You will usually receive a flyer from your school announcing the date, time and location of the college fair. If it's not at your school, it will typically be at a school or event center nearby.

Review the list of attendees, and if you haven't heard of one of the schools, take a moment to visit its website. Make notes about its location, number of students, majors, scholarship offerings and student organizations.

Circle the universities you'd like to learn more about at the fair. If you have specific questions, write them down so you'll remember to ask. It's a good idea to put those questions on your smart phone or iPad.

DURING THE COLLEGE FAIR: NETWORK, NETWORK, NETWORK

1. Review the list of colleges that will be at the fair.

2. When you get to the fair, pick up a map to find your best-fitting colleges.

3. Students should approach the representatives of the universities that interest them.

4. Ask about programs and scholarships that might be a good fit for you.

5. Your child should seek on site counselors. They will be available to help you determine the colleges that meet your requirements regarding majors and other areas of interest.

6. Determine what your college bound student can do to stand out.

7. Learn as much as you can about the campus. Don't just pick up literature. Ask questions.

An extra note for the Parent/Agent about asking questions at a college fair. Help your college bound student learn how to be more than just someone in the room. Give the rep info also. College representatives love to say that they are looking for reasons to accept your college bound student so have him or her prepared to ask intelligent questions about the school and its programs.

An extra note for the student/client. Stay in touch with the admissions rep without stalking. Stay in touch and ask the questions that maybe no one else is asking. Dive into the academics, to show that you can bring value to the college, how will you stand out.

Your college bound student should formulate questions on his or her own. The student can find a lot of information such as historical data, the type of student that typically gets accepted and what helped those students gain admittance. Start off with the best list and compile and compare. You and your college bound student should also have a secondary goal at these fairs. You both have to determine which colleges your student would like to visit. Ask a rep if they have programs that will bring students to the campus. Maybe you're an underrepresented demographic such as minorities, women, etc. Maybe there's a need for women enrolling in an engineering program, so there may be a push to get potential students to fill this void on campus.

The List

Here's a quick review of where you should be. Your child has earned decent grades, has established a relationship with the school's counselor, knows what he or she likes and has attended at least one college fair. You have reviewed application procedures, have a basic view of what financial aid will or will not be available and have a good idea of what to expect.

The next thing to do is for you and your child to sit and make a tentative college list. You both have enough information to start making a final list of prospective colleges. This can not be done in one session. In fact, your child may contact a counselor to get more specific information. You won't be able to get all the details about financial aid, but you should have a good idea. Create virtual and real folders to save brochures and other material which will help you learn more about the college campus, what it offers for class majors and other categories using the titles and subtitles from this book for ideas to name the folders you create.

The Visit

If you've planned well, you can incorporate college campus visits into vacations. Your child will quickly learn what he or she does or doesn't like. But for the comprehensive visit, you'll need to do a little more planning. That's why there's a separate segment dedicated to college campus visits in this chapter.

There are three types of visits. One is formal which will allow you to call ahead, meet a representative, talk to students, perhaps have your child sit in on a class and take a tour. The other is just a stroll through campus that will allow you child to see if he or she likes it. The third is taken by a high school student who has been accepted by a college or university.

The important thing is to maintain the connections you made at the college fair. Even if you end up not applying to a particular university, you will have found a resource you can trust. And no matter where you end up going, that's invaluable support.

FORMALLY VISITING A COLLEGE CAMPUS AND WHAT YOU SHOULD EXPECT TO LEARN FOR COLLEGE BOUND STUDENTS:

1. Make an appointment to take an official tour and informational session (schools may track your visits).

2. You will learn things about the school that you never knew (such as new majors and opportunities).

3. Does your student hate older buildings? Like a large campus? You'll find out during these visits.

4. You get the opportunity to make personal connections with admission representatives.

Visiting the college your child is considering is imperative. This gives your student a first-hand look at colleges and universities.

This is a perfect opportunity to learn what the college has to offer. It will give you a chance to experience the culture, obtain meetings with admissions representatives, participate in student led tours, and get to see campus housing. This helps to have a realistic picture of a school outside of a brochure or pictures on the internet.

Let me provide more motivation for making these visits. I've heard of too many stories of students seeing the campus for the first time when they arrive as a new student and not being happy with their decision when they realize the school isn't a good fit. By then it's too late. Money has been paid and there's no way to get it back.

I wouldn't recommend attending a school that you've never visited the campus. When you're making your decision to what school to attend you need to visit the campus. Look at this way. You wouldn't want your child to move into an apartment without seeing it. Take the same approach with attending college.

QUESTION THE PRODUCT:
Everyone you meet is there to give you the school's best face. It's your job to read between the lines.

Here are some questions you may want to ask your tour guide or students you meet on campus:

1. What are the best reasons to go to this college?
2. What's it like to go from high school to college?
3. What do you do in your free time? On the weekends?
4. What do you love about this college?
5. What do you wish you could change about this college?
6. Why did you choose this college?
7. What is it like to live here?

When you visit will determine how much you see. Here are some tips about what you can and can not see at specific times of year.

PLANNING THE VISIT:

Plan your visit in advance and make sure classes will be in session. Mondays through Thursdays are ideal for visits since campuses are generally in full swing.

- Visiting on a Friday may not be as practical, as students, faculty and staff might be busy with social activities starting Friday afternoon.

- High school holidays that fall on Mondays are often great opportunities for making college visits. Many colleges are in session on these days and you won't be missing any of your high school classes.

- The late summer and early September before senior year are convenient times to visit, since many colleges begin their fall semester as early as mid-August.

- The spring of junior year is a good time if you've already researched colleges.

- Spring break is also good if you play fall sports or are considering applying under early action or early decision plans.

- Seniors can also visit in the fall, that timing can help seniors narrow college lists.

Visiting a college campus is one of the most exciting steps in choosing a college. If possible, it's best to visit colleges before your applications are due. That way, you can be confident you'd be happy at any of the colleges you're applying to. It's also best to go is when the college is in session. That way, you'll get to see it when classes are meeting and day-to-day activities are taking place.

    Do not schedule a visit when the campus is deserted. Call the college or look on the college's website for the academic calendar to find out when breaks, reading periods and exam periods are scheduled.

WHAT TO INVESTIGATE DURING A FORMAL CAMPUS VISIT:

- Surrounding area
- Students on campus
- Resident halls
- Academics
- Facilities
- Dining halls

When your college bound student makes a formal campus visit as an accepted high school senior the stakes are very high. The school has made it clear your student is what they want. But your student will have to take on adult sized responsibility to see if he or she wants to attend that particular school.

THE ACCEPTED HIGH SCHOOL SENIOR VISIT:

My daughter was down to two schools and we went to the Accepted Student's Day to make the final choice. The environment played a large role in her decision. She had a chance to immerse herself in campus to see how well she would adjust.

All seniors should visit during an Accepted Students Day if possible. Questions and concerns will be addressed as the college provides your student with invaluable information that will guide him or her through a successful transition from high school to higher education. During the visit, the student will hear from campus students, faculty and staff, as they highlight the numerous opportunities available there. Looking at the students your child will be going to school with, gives them a feel of what it may be like. Usually these campus visits are offered early spring once you find out the college's decision.

When planning your campus visits, make sure to allow time to explore each college. While you're there, talk to as many people as possible. These can include college admission staff, professors and students. Below are some other things you can do while visiting. Note that some activities, such as meeting with an admission officer or staying overnight in a dorm, might need to be set up in advance.

VISITING CAMPUS AS AN ACCEPTED SENIOR:
- Attend a class
- Meet with a professor
- Meet with an admission officer
- Meet with a financial aid officer
- Attend a club meeting or a sports practice session
- Eat in the dining hall
- Spend the night in a dorm
- Gather information

- Take part in a group information session at the admission office
- Pick up financial aid forms
- Sit in on a class that interests you
- If classes aren't in session, just see what the classrooms are like
- Meet a professor who teaches a subject that interests you
- Talk to students about what they think of their classes and professors
- Get the names of the people you meet and their business cards so you can contact them later if you have questions
- Remember to take pictures of things that you might forget later
- Maximize the experience

The Parent/Agent should also assess the campus after the Accepted Student's Day. It is your job to make sure that a student isn't blinded by glitz or a school's reputation on paper. Even though your student is excited, make sure he or she also gathers facts.

Financial Aid

This is a core component of college. Money is available to help you pay for college, so don't rule out any college you like just because of its cost. Financial aid comes in different forms, grants and scholarships, which don't have to be re-paid; federal loans which generally carry a low interest rate and are repaid after you graduate or leave school; and employment, usually 10 to 15 hours per week. Most students receive a combination or "package" made up of all three types of aid based on "financial need." After you complete and submit a FAFSA form, colleges will send you an award letter indicating what types of aid you are eligible for.

THE FASFA FORM:

This form is EXTREMELY important. Many people think they shouldn't fill it out because they make too much money, but it's truly a determent to not fill it out. There is more information about this tool in chapter 6 of this book.

For example, a Parent Plus federal loan will give you a completive interest rate and lets you borrow up to the cost of attendance, but you must fill out a FASFA form. If you want/need your student to get a loan as well, they can as they aren't based on income. The students are giving the info, but the parents are usually the ones to complete. Keep in mind it's the student filling out the form so the students assets weigh heavenly to what they can contribute to their own education as compared to the parents. However, for a federal student loan, a FAFSA must be completed.

CSS (COLLEGE SCHOLARSHIP SERVICES PROFILE):

The CSS (College Scholarship Services Profile) is a form filled out to help you obtain financial aid, but it's only for private schools. It's an application you have to pay for and some colleges will require you to have this completed. They get more in-depth as to what your finances look like. Again, in chapter 6 there is more information about this form.

FINDING SCHOLARSHIPS:

Many scholarships want someone who is involved in community, has a cause they are passionate about and have a specified GPA. Colleges are often hard pressed to find the kids that are involved in the community. It isn't just about grades even though they are a factor but each scholarship has different requirements based on their goals.

There are several different types of scholarships. Encourage your children to apply for whatever scholarships you can. Several high schools will have scholarship programs from different organizations, often our top students don't get these because they may be looking for something different than grades.

An easier way for a parent to get scholarship money is through the school/college themselves. We found more opportunities at the school level-based on grades (merit awards).

My daughter was able to get money from a lot of schools but of course not from the one she wanted to go to, I guess that's just how it works out sometimes.

Let me provide a couple of examples. One college might say: "Give us a student that's majoring in early childhood education and they get free tuition." Or here's another, "You play the cello and we really want a cello player." If you child loves cello he or she gets money for school by simply doing something he or she likes.

The Talk: Part II

It's often a full time job looking at opportunities for your children. I didn't want to pay too much for programs so we focused on finding opportunities.

Research is key when finding your best-fit school, and it's crucial to leave no stone unturned. While it's important to become familiar with a school's website and to physically visit the campus if you can, social media outlets are effective supplemental research tools. Arming yourself with all the information possible will help you develop a college list that meets all of your interests and needs. To learn more about any college on your list, check its College Profile. Be sure to confirm application requirements directly with each college to which you apply.

But after the searching, surfing, visiting and filling out applications your child will have to understand that a large part of the payment process will be placed on his or her shoulders. Unfortunately, many college students graduate with a staggering amount of debt that will plague them for years because they didn't understand the repayment programs tied to colleges.

Then there's also the factor of college graduation rates. Many students enter college with the assumption that they will graduate within four years. However, that is not the case for a significant number of undergrads. The national 6-year graduation rate for individuals seeking a 4-year degree is 59%. There are penalties attached to students to take time away from school and still have loans. Make sure you understand all of the ramifications of the forms you sign and make sure your college bound student know the financial obligations that come with attending college.

Chapter Five

How a School Screens Your Child

● ●

This chapter will explain how schools screen your child:

▶ PSAT

▶ SAT

▶ ACT

▶ Essays Misc

▶ Recommendations

▶ Diversity Misc

● ●

AGENT POV:
It's easier to make your student comply when they see the results.

PARENT POV:
Remember there's a thin line between being irritating and getting noticed.

"Life is like a combination lock; your job is to find the right numbers, in the right order, so you can have anything you want"

– Brian Tracy

*W*e have all experienced the following situation. You walk into a room and the people who are already there watch you. They watch how you move. They listen to how you speak. They are judging and screening you. Unfortunately, we don't always know what standards are used to rate us in other circumstances. But when it comes to the college selection process the standards, in most instances, are known. Your child is being screened by the universities and colleges he or she wants to attend. For that reason, you need to start building a resume of accomplishments. Schools will judge your child's high school transcripts, of course. However, few college students gain admittance based on grades alone. Some schools require essays, others expect recommendations from adults who know the student. Most colleges and universities also expect to see your child's SAT or ACT scores.

Both of these college entrance exams are daunting. Some students have test anxiety and do poorly on them. For that reason there is the PSAT. It lets your student know what to expect.

SAT

SAT scores help students find a good college match. Colleges have different levels of competitiveness and different definitions of what a "good" score is. Here are some basic SAT facts:

PSAT

This is a practice version of the SAT taken during the 10th and 11th grades. To learn more about it visit collegboard.org for tips and strategies. Test prep companies like Kaplan and Princeton Review may also offer full length practice ACT exams, as well as, SAT full length practice exams.

1. Cost (2015-2016) $43.00 with out essay and $54.50 with essay

2. Registration Online at collegeboard.org

3. SAT given October, November, December, January, March, May and June

SAT Score Reporting

1. There is one score report for all the tests taken unless you use the score choice option where you can select specific scores from a testing date.

2. It takes three weeks to receive scores. (For the first administration of the redesigned SAT – March 2016 it will take longer to receive scores)

3. Total Score: Evidence-Based Reading and Writing and Mathematics 400-1600

4. Evidenced-Based Reading and Writing 200–800

5. Mathematics 200–800

6. Optional Essay 2-8 Essay (rubric is based on a better and writing). This is reported separately.

There are additional scores that will give the student a better idea of the child's specific strengths and weaknesses in various academic areas. Some students take the SAT more than once.

1. Test scores *3 scores*: reading, writing, language and math - range 10-40

2. Cross test scores *2 scores*: analysis in science and analysis in history/social studies - range 10-40

3. Sub-scores *7 scores*: words in context, heart of algebra, command of evidence, passport to advanced mathematics, expression of ideas, problem solving and data analysis, and standard English conventions - range 1-15

If you or your child feel that additional preparation help is needed the following information will help.

SAT Prep Classes

- School sponsored classes

- Private organizations – Kaplan and Princeton Review

- Use www.Khanacademy.com as a prep tool

- SAT Question of the day – available on collegeboard.com

- Visit collegeboard.org for tips and strategies for taking the SAT

ACT

ACT test questions are directly related to what is taught in high school.

1. English – 75 questions, 45 minutes to take test

2. Reading – 40 questions, 35 minutes to take test

3. Math – 60 questions, 60 minutes to take test

4. Science – 40 questions, 35 minutes to take test

5. ACT Writing Section Optional Section (additional fee)
   - Essay – 30 minutes to take test
   - The essay consists of one writing prompt that describes two points of view on an issue and students are asked to write response.

ACT facts:

- Cost (2015-2016) $39.50

- ACT Plus Writing $56.50

- ACT is given September, October, December, February, April and June.

- Visit www.act.org frequently

ACT Score Reporting:

- Scores include: each test score (English, Math, Reading, Science)

- Scores range from 1 (low) to 36 (high)

- Composite Score which is the average of your four test scores, rounded to the nearest whole number.

- Separate report for each time test is taken

- Takes 2 ½ weeks to receive scores

How to Prepare for ACT:

1. Take rigorous courses in a strong curriculum

2. Read and write extensively in and out of school

3. Review books

4. You may want your child to take ACT prep courses with a test prep company

5. Visit www.act.org frequently for tips and strategies for taking the ACT exam

Essays

The Perfect College Essay

Most selective colleges require you to submit an essay or personal statement as part of your application. It may sound like a chore, and it will certainly take some work. But it's also a great opportunity that can make a difference at decision time. Admissions committees put the most weight on your high school grades, rigor of courses and your test scores. However, selective colleges receive applications from many worthy students with similar scores and grades—too many to admit. So they use your essay, along with your letters of recommendation and extracurricular activities to find out what sets you apart from the other talented candidates.

Identify what sets your child apart. Maybe they have a unique background or want to share their interests and personality. This is their chance to tell their story. The best way to tell their story is to write a personal, thoughtful essay about something that has meaning for them. When they are honest and genuine, their unique qualities will shine through. Colleges want to know the real you. When you apply to colleges, you don't have to try to make yourself look better by listing the kinds of accomplishments or writing the kind of essay you think they want to see. If you're honest about who you are and what you've done, you're more likely to end up at a college that's a good fit for you.

Admissions reps have to read an unbelievable number of essays, most of which are forgettable. Many students try to sound smart rather than sounding like themselves or share information that isn't relative. Others write about a subject that they don't care about, but that they think will impress admissions. Colleges are simply looking for thoughtful, motivated students who will add something to the class.

Have your student write about something that's important to him or her. It could be an experience, a person, a book–anything that has had an impact on your child's life. When recalling these events, the students need to give more than the play–by–play or just state facts. Have them describe what they learned from the experience and how it changed them.

Start early and write several drafts. Set it aside for a few days and read it again. Put yourself in the shoes of an admissions reps: Is the essay interesting? Do the ideas flow logically? Does it reveal something about the applicant? Is it written in the applicant's own voice?

What's written in the application essay or personal statement should not contradict any other part of your application. This isn't the place to list your awards or discuss your grades or test scores.

If there is a question and answer section, answer the question being asked. Don't reuse an answer to a similar question from another application.

Have at least one other person edit your essay. A teacher or college counselor is your best resource. And before you send it off, check, check again, and then triple check to make sure your essay is free of spelling or grammar errors.

The deadline for regular decision applications is normally between January 1 and February 1, depending on the college. Get the bulk of your essays done early fall and confirm who will write your recommendations, so you won't have a lot of last-minute work to do during the holiday season.

Recommendations

When you apply to college, you will typically submit between one and three recommendation letters from teachers, counselors, employers and/or other adults who can vouch for your academic achievements or personal character. Even though others actually write the letters, you might be surprised to discover that you can influence the results by who you select and what information you provide them.

In college admissions, application forms and essays give admissions officers your own perspective on your achievements. However, to get another person's viewpoint they often turn to your letters of recommendation.

You want people who can testify in support of your strengths, who are believable, and who won't reveal anything incriminating. Essentially you want to find people who know your strengths and will attest to them. Choose the one who knows you and your accomplishments best. Once you select recommenders write him or her a cover letter or send an email to make a formal request to write a recommendation for you.

If the application has a specific teacher recommendation form, give this form to the recommender who will email or mail (provide envelope with college address and stamps) to college when it is completed. In most cases, this is now done online with the application. If that is the case, you will need to provide the teacher's name and email address. Make sure you are entering the correct email address for your teachers. If you enter it incorrectly they will not receive the information and will not be able to submit their recommendation.

It's a good idea to remind the teacher what class you had with them, what your final grade was, and what topic you particularly enjoyed in the class. Be sure to include this information in the cover letter, and a list of all the deadlines.

Diversity

It's a struggle for many especially small private schools to get diversity on campus so there may be incentives and help to get them enrolled. Identify the initiative the college has and the gaps that they need to fill to determine how you may be able to not just fit into the mix but stand out.

When we began looking for the right fit for our daughter we visited a college in Pennsylvania and realized there was no diversity whatsoever. My daughter immediately realized this wasn't where she wanted to be. This speaks to your child knowing themselves and being exposed to explore environments where they fit. Sometimes you may have to face the realization that although the college may have a good program for your child, they probably won't matriculate well there.

Verdel A. Jones

Chapter Six

Finding the Money vs. Biting the Bullet and Saving

• •

This chapter will explore options for paying for college:

▶ Financial Aid Forms

▶ Federal Sources

▶ Private Sources

▶ Specialized Funds

▶ Financial Aid Resources

▶ Net Price Calculator

• •

AGENT POV:

You must keep track of and control the schedule, or it will control you.

PARENT POV:

Start saving for college as soon as possible. Later sounds great, but comes quickly.

"Money isn't everything, but it sure keeps you in touch with your children."

~J. Paul Getty

*C*ollege isn't cheap. For many families, the cost of college can be daunting. You may want to start off by discussing the cost of college and what you plan to or are able to contribute from the start and going forward. Financial professionals typically recommend that parents avoid promising to pay 100% of college costs, in case they experience an unforeseeable financial setback or maybe you are like my husband and I who didn't get an early start, so we had to play catch up.

We should have been all the way in, but this is one of the things I would do differently. I would save for college. We didn't because we never thought the time was right, but what we were doing was wasting time. We could have saved a little here and there, we didn't but we could have. Now we're faced with this large debt. Remember it all adds up and you don't have as much time as you're telling yourself.

When we finally woke up we realized we were late. We had to get a plan together quickly as time was running short. My husband and I had agreed that we would do whatever we needed to do to make sure our children went to college. This was the commitment my husband and I made to each other and our children.

Without certain loans college would have been a struggle and sometimes impossible for many without this funding. We explained to our kids that they are going to have to contribute to help us pay back some of the loans we took out, once they are established in their profession.

We had the conversation and it was real, just as it needs to be. We laid out the options to both of our children, "If you go to this school we/you won't have to have loans, but if you go to this college you will because this college is $45,000 a year for example." By having that discussion with them we set the expectation and were real about what was possible.

The next set of facts I am sharing with you seem like they have nothing to do with money. It's a list of deadlines. After you read through them I'll explain why they're in this chapter

COLLEGE APPLICATION DEADLINES

Every university and college has its own application deadlines, but they fall around the same time. There are lots of important questions every college bound student and his or her Parent/ Agent should ask, but one of the most important is, "When is the deadline?" Knowing the important dates when your information must be submitted is crucial. Turning in information late can hurt your child's chances of being admitted or receiving funds for college.

- Early Applicants (early action, early decision or single choice early action) generally need to get their applications in by either November 1 or November 15.

- Some colleges and universities have rolling admissions. There is no specific deadline. Colleges review applications as they come in and make decisions within a few weeks after review. However, once they fill up the freshman class they may not admit any more students. The key with rolling admissions is to apply early. The later in the application process, the more stringent the admittance criteria.

- Some schools ask that supplemental material be submitted with your application. Sometimes you can send it a couple of weeks after the application deadline. And a few even want supplemental material sent before the actual application. It's best to check with each school to see what the requirements are.

- May 1 is Universal deposit day. All colleges want the deposit. This is next step toward bringing you closer to accomplishing your goal.

- Financial Aid FASFA form submission January 1 (for the class of 2017 beyond – October 1 is the beginning filing date).

Not having all of your admission materials submitted on time may wind up making everything else null and void. Be prepared. Have your application materials ready before the last minute. That's the only way to avoid a lot of stress come deadline day.

Now why are these deadlines financially important? Because they take a lot of time and effort. You can focus so much on essays and forms that you miss the deadline for scholarships and financial aid. SCHEDULE TIME weekly and get the college tuition payment in on time. Without it your student can get kicked out of his or her first day of class.

Some of the information listed below is briefly described in a previous chapter. But this segment provides more information about where to find the funds that will pay the high cost of a college education.

Financial Aid Forms
Forms You Need to Complete for Financial Aid

- Free Application For Federal Student Aid - FAFSA - use to submit your application. www.fafsa.gov

- Federal Student Aid ID (FSA ID) - gives you access to Federal Student Aid's online systems and can serve as your legal signature. www.fsaid.ed.gov/npas/index.htm

Some of this information was described briefly in the previous chapter. It's here again in more detail because it's important enough to list twice.

THE FASFA FORM

You may be asking why fill it out if I know I make too much money for federal aid? But ignore it at your own financial risk.

Many colleges use it to award institutional aid dollars (private dollars that the college can award at their own discretion) too.

Federal loans such as the Parent Plus Loan will give you a competitive interest rate and lets you borrow up to the cost of attendance, but you must fill out a FASFA form. If you want/ need your student to get a federal loan, the FAFSA must be completed. Both of these options are not based on income. The students are giving the info, but the parents are usually the ones completing this form. Keep in mind it's the student filling out the form so the student's assets weigh heavenly to what they can contribute to their own education as compared to the parents.

When the federal government receives the form and looks at the calculation to determine how much you can pay for college they will take a closer look at the student to see what they can contribute based on savings, assets etc. in addition to the parent's income, assets and other financial information. That EFC (Expected Family Contribution) is the actual dollar amount you can pay for college. The government recently changed the guidelines for when people can apply. Instead of January of senior year, you will be able to apply as early as October. What happened traditionally, you'd fill out the financial aid form in January using the previous year tax returns. Since no one has filed taxes in January, you would have to follow up and update the records when you filed your taxes in the following year. Now students will have a considerable amount of time to gather appropriate tax documents. They will be able to use "prior-prior year" taxes and data.

THE CSS PROFILE FORM

The CSS (College Scholarship Services Profile) is a form filled out to help you obtain financial aid, but it's only for private schools. It's an application you have to pay for and some colleges will require you to have this completed. They get more in-depth as to what your finances look like.

Federal Sources
THE PELL GRANT

A Federal Pell Grant, unlike a loan, does not have to be repaid. Federal Pell Grants usually are awarded only to undergraduate students who have not earned a bachelor's or a professional degree. This grant is need based.

WORK STUDY

Federal Work-Study provides part-time jobs for undergraduate and graduate students with financial need, allowing them to earn money to help pay educational expenses. The program encourages community service work and work related to the student's course of study. It will be included as a part of the Financial Aid awards package.

You have the option to accept it or not. When filling out your FASFA form it will ask you if you want to be considered for work study. If you feel like you will need to supplement their tuition this is a great way to do it, However, this program is need based.

FEDERAL LOANS

The Direct Parent Plus Loan: is a loan credit worthy parents can apply for. They can borrow up to the cost of attendance as determined by each school. These loans are not need based. Student Loans: Direct Subsidized Loans are loans made to eligible undergraduate students who demonstrate financial need to help cover the costs of higher education at a college or career school.

Student Loans: Direct Unsubsidized Loans are loans made to eligible undergraduate, graduate, and professional students, but in this case, the student does not have to demonstrate financial need to be eligible for the loan.

Private Sources

Many scholarships want to award students who are involved in the community, have a cause they are passionate about and have

Ways to Finance College:

1. Scholarships

2. Completing the FAFSA form

3. College Affordability and Transparency Center

4. http://collegecost.ed.gov/

5. www.fastweb.com

6. Fastweb.com the scholarship opportunities come to you

a B+ GPA. Colleges are often hard pressed to find the kids that are involved in the community. It isn't just about grades even though they are a factor but each scholarship has different requirements based on their goals. They specialize in a specific area. Knowing that will help you narrow your focus.

SCHOOL SCHOLARSHIPS

An easier way to get scholarship money is through the school/ college themselves. If your student has good grades and/or SAT or ACT scores, they may receive merit based scholarships. Most colleges will indicate if you've received this type of award in the acceptance letter. However, you can research the criteria for merit based scholarships on college websites. In addition, colleges have other types of scholarships based on majors, community involvement and other criteria.

SCHOLARSHIPS FROM ORGANIZATIONS

Several groups, clubs and organizations also offer scholarships to involved students, which is another reason to make sure your students are actively involved in things that colleges see as valuable. A lot of these scholarships can be done by nomination and your school counselor may be the one to nominate you. You have to be strategic when applying for scholarships. Finding money for college is a lot of work and you have to have cooperation from your children to write essays. For our daughter it was not an issue because she's a journalist at heart, but for my son that part was a struggle. Knowing your child is always a factor.

PERSONAL LOANS

Personal Student Loans can help supply the necessary funds to fully complete a workable college fund. Personal loans can help students meet their outstanding tuition costs, as well as provide funds for various additional expenses such as room and board, computers, books and related college necessities.

Before considering any personal or private student loans, it is important to first exhaust all other forms of financial aid. This cannot be stressed enough. Many a student has been undone by taking on more debt than they can handle, and it is vital to restrict borrowing, particularly private sector borrowing, to an absolute minimum.

Financial Aid Resources

FAFSA4caster - The FAFSA4caster will help you understand your options for paying for college, provide some basic information and will estimate your eligibility for federal student aid. https://studentaid.ed.gov/sa/fafsa/estimate

We knew we wouldn't get financial aid based on need because we had filled out the financial aid forecaster, which you can begin filling out in the 9th grade to get your EFC (Expected Family Contribution). This is an important tool to see what you can contribute. If it says your EFC is $10,000 and the cost of attendance is $40,000 some colleges will meet that need with a combination of things, work study, financial aid, loans etc., but you want to attempt to find a college that will meet that need with a loan being your last option. Your finances might change from year to year, but if they are pretty much the same you'll have a good snapshot of the need that must be met.

CATC – The College Affordability and Transparency Center

The CATC was designed by the U.S. Department of Education to meet requirements in the Higher Education Opportunity Act to provide better information to student and parents about college costs. It compares college tuition and fees, net price, and other characteristics.

Fastweb.com - a search service that matches skills, abilities, and interests to a database of more than 400,000 scholarships. www.fastweb.com

FinAid - information on financial aid and scholarship search. www.finaid.org

FinAid Award Letter Comparison Tool - helps you compare and contrast the financial aid packages from the colleges that have admitted you. In particular, it highlights differences in the cost of attending each school. www.finaid.org/calculators/ awardletter.phtml

FinAid Reduced or No Loans - This link includes a table of colleges that have taken steps to significantly reduce or eliminate the self-help level or eliminate loans from the aid package for lower income students. www.finaid.org/questions/ noloansforlowincome.phtml

FinAid Veterans and Dependent Scholarships – list information on educational assistance for relatives of veterans. www.finaid.org/military/veterans.phtml

National Association of Student Financial Aid Administrators
NASFAA provides professional development to financial aid administrators to help students gain access to higher education. This helpful link details all of the financial aid programs available by state to help pay for college. www.nasfaa.org/ students/state_financial_aid_programs.aspx

Net Price Calculator

You can find this calculator on the colleges site to determine the cost of college attendance for your child. The cost of attendance includes: tuition, room and board, fees, travel, books and miscellaneous expenses. This calculator takes into account your GPA, ACT and/or SAT scores, community involvement and income, to determine the net price you will pay to attend that school. Good grades and high college entrance scores, may yield you merit scholarships based on academics. The Net Price Calculator gives you a good snapshot/estimate on what you need to pay for college for the first year.

Verdel A. Jones

Chapter Seven

Apply and Begin the Waiting Game

● ●

This chapter will explain how the waiting game works:

▶ The Application

▶ At How Many Schools Should Your Child Apply?

▶ College Application Options

▶ Multiple Submission Websites

▶ Submission Fees and Waivers

▶ Schools with Division I and Division II Requirements

▶ Getting Accepted

▶ The Move

▶ How to Handle College Rejections

▶ Postponing a Higher Education

▶ Community Colleges

● ●

AGENT POV:

Make sure your child celebrates the closing of a life chapter (and opening of a new one).

PARENT POV:

All transitions have peaks and valleys.

"All that is valuable in human society depends upon the opportunity for development accorded the individual."

~ Albert Einstein

*B*efore you and your student can rest…you have to apply. Here are a few tools to get your applications completed. Once that is completed there is nothing left for you, and your student, to do but wait.

The Application

Once you have created a list of colleges to apply to based on all of the research you and your student have completed, it is time to actually apply. Refer back to the 12th grade timeline and checklist in chapter 3 for specific tasks. Staying organized will make the application process go smoothly and help you meet deadlines by keeping track of the college application requirements and tasks that are still outstanding. Use the list below to check off important tasks that need to be complete for each college application.

ORGANIZING YOURSELF and YOUR STUDENT: THE APPLICATION CHECKLIST

College: _____

_____ Get the application (find out the method of application submission – most are online)

_____ Make a note of the regular application deadline

_____ Make a note of the early application deadline

_____ Have your child request recommendation letters

_____ Have your child draft initial essay

_____ Proofread essay for spelling and grammar

_____ Have two people read your child's essay

_____ Have your child revise the essay

_____ Proofread the revision

_____ Complete all parts of the application, submit and pay fee or use fee wavier

_____ Request that your child's high school transcript be sent

_____ Make copies of all application materials

_____ Tell school counselor that you applied

_____ Confirm receipt of application materials

_____ Have your child send thank you notes to recommendation writers

There are also fee waivers available. Ask colleges if they give fee waivers.

_____ Make a note of the priority financial aid deadline

_____ Make a note of the regular financial aid deadline

_____ Submit FAFSA

_____ Submit CSS Profile, if needed

_____ Submit college aid form, if needed

_____ Submit state aid form, if needed

_____ Receive letter from office of admission

_____ Receive financial aid award letter

_____ Meet deadline (usually May 1) to accept admission and send deposit

_____ Notify the colleges your child will not attend by sending an email to admissions to free up space for other students

_____ Accept financial aid offer

_____ Find out if a placement exam is required

_____ Take AP or IB exams given in May

_____ Send AP scores if applicable – scores are available in July

Here's another tip. Keep the following eight pieces of information at your finger tips. This will help when filling out the applications.

- Your child's Social Security number

- Your child's high school CEEB (College Entrance Examination Board) Code

- A copy of your child's high school transcript

- Your child's activity/resume

- Your college bound child's score report from a college admission test (SAT/ACT)

- Parent or legal guardian information

- High School address and phone number

- Name of recommenders and correct email information and school counselor contact information

Applying to college is a big job, but you can make it easier by breaking it down into a series of small steps. Students should submit online applications via the Internet. It is the standard procedure for colleges and there are several ways to obtain a college's application electronically.

If you do want a paper copy of an application, you can find them in the admissions office of each institution.

If you want or need to mail an application, or the school requires it, it's strongly advised that you get delivery confirmation for your applications and a receipt to prove you mailed it on time, in case something goes wrong.

The college application deadlines generally mean that you must have your application postmarked by that day – it doesn't necessarily have to be received by then. Check with the college you are applying to in order to confirm this.

Remember: It's always better to not wait until the last minute regardless!

At How Many Schools Should Your Child Apply?

We established the 6 college process in our home. Each one of my children applied to 6 colleges. They applied for two colleges in each of the three categories below.

DREAM COLLEGES - I called these dream colleges because they were a stretch, either because of cost or criteria. But they were good fits, nonetheless.

SAFETY COLLEGE – These are schools where our children met all the target requirements. Because they met the criteria, we felt it was a safe bet they would be accepted.

TARGET - These colleges fell between the DREAM and the SAFETY schools.

College Application Options
EARLY DECISION

When your child applies early decision, they are stating that this is his or her number one choice and they apply early in the fall (usually by November 1) of the senior year. If accepted, they must attend if offered admission. Upon acceptance, students must withdraw their applications at other colleges. Decisions are given to applicants in mid-December. If not accepted under the early decision, a student is often reconsidered (deferred) for admission later in the senior year. This option is rare.

EARLY ACTION

Early action follows the same application/notification timetable as early decision but does not obligate the candidate to accept the offer of admission. Students can apply to other colleges and do not have to make a decision until the spring. This option shows that a student is serious about a certain college and gets the application process out of the way early.

SPRING NOTIFICATION

Colleges who use spring notification have application deadlines from January 1 to February 15. Decisions are mailed to applicants from early to mid-April and the accepted applicants are required to notify the college they choose to attend not later than May 1. There are several variations to this process with some schools using a variety of deadline dates and reply deadlines.

ROLLING ADMISSIONS

A college using rolling admissions reviews applications as they come in and returns decisions within a few weeks after review. The key to this option is apply early. The longer you wait the tougher it might be to get accepted into the college.

Multiple Submission Websites

Another way to apply to colleges that is very commonly used is the Common Application. The Common Application is one application that more than 600 colleges and universities participate in. You can apply to multiple colleges on one application which saves you time. With this process, you go to www.commonapp.org, fill out the application and indicate which colleges you want the application sent to. It's very easy and efficient. Keep in mind that although you are only filling out one application, you still need to pay the application fee for each school you are applying to.

*You can visit **commonapp.org** to find out which colleges accept the Common Application.*

Submission Fees and Waivers

Several colleges have moved towards sending students free applications in the mail based on information obtained from PSAT and/or SAT data. Be sure to take advantage of this opportunity because applications can cost upwards of $60.00 each.

College application fee waivers are a great way to save money when you're applying to college. If you're eligible for college application fee waivers, you'll receive them in the fall of your senior year. Not every school accepts application fee waivers. Search for colleges that accept application fee waivers, and get ready to apply.

Every income-eligible senior who takes the SAT or SAT Subject Test using a fee waiver will receive four college application fee waivers from the College Board which may be used to apply to 2,000 participating colleges. Additionally, as part of the College Board's Access to Opportunity initiative, select students will receive college application fee waivers.

To have a college application fee waived, students must submit their fee waiver to the college they are applying to.

Most colleges and universities define eligibility for a college application fee waiver as being eligible for or having received a fee waiver for a test such as the SAT or an SAT Subject Test, participating in the National School Lunch Program, or receiving public assistance.

Before using a fee waiver, students should check to see if the college will accept it. Colleges that cooperate with the SAT Fee-Waiver Service are not obligated to waive their application fees, and some may require additional information before considering or granting a college application fee waiver.

Schools with Division 1 and Division II Requirements

Find out NCAA (National Collegiate Athletic Association) requirements if you want to play sports in college. If you visit the NCAA Eligibility Center at http://web3.ncaa.org/ECWR2/NCAA_EMS/NCAA.jsp you will learn more.

Getting Accepted

First of all, congratulate yourself on a job well done. Remember, though, that you didn't accomplish this feat all on your own. Don't check out. Remember, the college or university is still keenly interested in your child's grades and conduct for the remainder of the senior year. So, yes, he or she still needs to study for final exams.

Another important step is to show some courtesy to the colleges where your child doesn't intend to enroll, but has been accepted. There are deferred applicants who are itching to get off the wait list.

The Move

Encourage your child not to bring all of his or her stuff from their room at home. Our son loves movies, comics and video games. His first year of school it seemed as if he brought every single one he owned. Year two, he didn't. He was so busy with college activities that he barely had time to use any of it. Lesson learned - leave "stuff" at home.

There are some great websites that include great checklist of items you need to bring to college.

- Dormsmart.com
- Pinterest.com (search - college dorm checklist)

College Move Checklist

It's an exciting time. Sometimes we can forget something minor or crucial because we're so excited, nervous, scared or in shock. Here's a checklist of some things you should make sure you've completed before heading off to college:

The Move Check List

_____ Open up bank accounts before your child moves and try to identify other banks affiliated with yours

_____ Talk about what it might feel like to be away from home. Discuss both excitement and trepidation

_____ Help your student child apply for a credit card and talk to them about responsible use of it

_____ Talk about budgets

_____ Make sure he or she knows how to do laundry and cook a few staple items

_____ Talk about alcohol and drugs

_____ Buy him or her a good alarm clock and make sure he or she can get moving in the morning alone

_____ Make sure your financial aid has gone through

_____ Check the status on your FAFSA online and call your school's financial aid office to ensure your loans, grants or scholarships have processed

_____ Sign up for freshman or transfer orientation, which will likely occur right before the semester starts. Orientations vary by school

_____ Meet other students specifically the college roommate

_____ Discuss classes and majors with academic advisors

_____ Register for classes (if you haven't already)

_____ Learn about campus resources

_____ Buy an Ethernet cable. Your dorm may have Wi-Fi, or you may have your own Wi-Fi network, but connecting directly to the Internet with an Ethernet cable may mean faster and more secure Internet

_____ Check on all scheduled classes to make sure your student is enrolled properly and none were cancelled

_____ Buy dorm accessories

_____ Verify that the dorm room or apartment is ready

_____ Double check that you're all set up

How to Handle College Rejections

You must give some thought to how you will respond to possible rejection letters. What will you say? How will you handle it? Don't talk to your student about this yet, but your first reaction if that letter should come, can help your student keep perspective and deal with it. Be prepared.

Rejection isn't always a bad thing. Sometimes it sets your student up for another opportunity that may be a better fit. The key is to look at the bright side of the situation (even though it may be hard for your student to see right now). Allow yourself some time to be disappointed. The emotion is appropriate and real, so don't ignore it. Don't take it personally. Remember that not getting in these days is not an embarrassment, just a reflection of a process that is not personal. Their oversight in judgment is not your fault.

Make sure your student is prepared for all outcomes and realizes a decline letter isn't the end of the world.

Postponing a Higher Education

Not everyone wants to graduate from high school and immediately enroll in college. If you have a child like that, try to understand his or her reasons and then make them see that living with you and having no responsibilities is also not an option.

However, children who go to work in devastated areas of the world, take a year studying something exotic or just work and save money aren't doing anything wrong. Help them find their way. But don't enable them to drift.

Community Colleges

There are many reasons to attend a community college. Some of them are financial. Sometimes it's to raise a lackluster GPA. Or perhaps a community college offers the course level needed to get into a specific field, such as being a dental hygienist. You should know your child, if you've spent time showing your child the powers of discovery learning, your child should know himself or herself.

The other advantage of attending a community college is the living arrangements. Most students who attend college locally continue to live at home. That helps budgets and also ushers in a transition between parent and child as adults.

A couple of final notes. Your student can still get a scholarship to the college of their choice after going to community college. It even increases the odds of being accepted to a school they may not have been accepted to before so it can help them in many ways. But make sure the credits can transfer.

Let me close by saying that you can't push a student into arenas where they don't want to compete. Allow me to provide this one last example from my days as an educator.

We used to hold these Senior in Jeopardy meetings in January of each school year in my district. I would talk to the parents and let them know their child may not graduate. I'm not focusing on the parent, rather the child because the parent has done all he or she needs to do or can do. The children made their own decisions at this point and had set a path. If he/she hasn't done what was needed by this time, it's a problem. At this point it's up to the child to determine if they will show up academically.

Verdel A. Jones

Resources

Web links and a final word from a graduated son and enrolled daughter

● ●

This chapter will provide insight and resources:

▶ Letter from author's daughter

▶ Letter from author's son

▶ Resource URLs

● ●

"At the end of the day, the most overwhelming key to a child's success is the positive involvement of parents."

~ Jane D. Hull

*W*e had to change a lot of things in our lives to represent our children, as far as our schedules were concerned. When you have kids that are involved, you are primarily doing things for them. Adult activities take a back seat. That was our perspective as Parent/Agents. So to end this book, I asked them to write what they remembered, honestly, about our Parent/Agent approach to their plans for college. Both of the letters are edited, but what touches me is they understood the love that motivated our intense family schedules. I hope you see that in the words on this page. I certainly see it in their lives.

A Letter from a grateful daughter

My parents/agents have always encouraged me to do what I loved. I think more importantly they have never discouraged me. They were always very encouraging and never looked at me as if I was crazy for wanting to do what I wanted to do. I heard nothing but good things from them when I wanted to pursue something, whether it was in sports or academics. They never questioned my ability to do it.

Growing up, I thought college was a huge place that adults went to get educated on the world. I knew that I was going to go because my parents always set that expectation for both me and my brother. I've always done fairly well in school and believed that I could make it in college, when the time came.

I've always wanted to go to college because I thought it was the standard. It was a given that I would attend and I did not want to try anything that steered away from that path because I did not know what other way there was to go. It seemed like the best option for me.

My parents have always set high expectations and because of that I realize that if you expect great things from someone, they have a better chance of achieving those goals.

There are many things that my parents have taught me over the years. But the main thing that always stayed with me is that family is important and for me, is the foundation for a happy life.

We gave our son the flexibility to gain his independence and it paid off. Rather than enable him we gave him space to develop into a strong young man.

Letter from a grateful son

I was an impressionable kid, I picked up things from who I was around like responsibility and independence. I always wanted to go to college. It seemed like the next step to do more stuff and go beyond what you saw. The lesson I learned from my parents that resonates with me mostly, is treat others with respect and learn to handle your business. Many kids my age didn't want to put in the work required to get things done. But my parents pushed this point really hard until it was engrained in me. It has helped me get through many things and move on when other kids got left behind

My K-12 education taught me how to read, write and work. I learned independence, confidence and responsibility from my parents through the things they exposed me to. Observing and thinking became second nature. By watching the people around me, seeing them happy and successful I'd try to emulate that.

The role my parents played had a big impact. We visited a lot of colleges to learn what I liked and visited a lot of colleges to learn what I didn't like. I used all those resources to make the right decision for me.

My mother also taught me the importance of having valuable things on my high school resume that would get attention, so I would look good to the colleges I was interested in. Ultimately, my parents represented me well and helped me to get to where I am today, a productive member of society, working in my field and enjoying life.

Resources

COLLEGE SEARCH WEBSITES

Campus Tours www.CampusTours.com - a source for virtual college tours, with interactive campus maps, videos, photographs and live cameras.

CollegeBoard www.collegeboard.org/ – CollegeBoard, the company that creates the SAT has a college search option. Look for the college search tab.

CollegeNet www.collegenet.com - a site for finding colleges, scholarships and financial aid, touring campuses virtually, and completing applications online, with links to related information.

CollegeData www.collegedata.com - serves as an online college advisor. This site contains information on preparing for the college process an excellent one stop shopping.

CollegeView www.collegeview.com - profiles of more than 3,700 colleges and universities, virtual tours of hundreds of schools, career planning tools, financial information and even advice in packing for college, and student blogs.

Peterson's Education & Career Center www.petersons.com/ - information colleges and universities. Helpful articles related to the college application progress.

Princeton Review www.review.com – go to the find your college tool that contains thousands of college profiles, best 380 rankings and expert advice from top counselors.

U.S. News Online Colleges & Careers Center www.usnews.com - "best value" rankings of colleges and graduate programs in multiple fields, with related information on careers and financial aid. Found in the education section of the website.

COLLEGE TEST PREP

ACT www.actstudent.org/testprep/ – ACT is the company that creates the ACT exam and they provide information on test preparation.

CollegeBoard www.collegeboard.org/ – CollegeBoard, the company that creates the PSAT and SAT exams has sample questions, free full length PSAT and SAT practice tests and paid resources including an online course and study guide.

Khan Academy www.khanacademy.org/ – free online tutoring for virtually every subject and free college test preparation.

Kaplan Online www.kaplan.com – will help you locate prep courses to prepare for college admission exams.

Peterson's Education & Career Center www.petersons.com/ - information on college test prep and free online practice tests.

Princeton Review www.review.com – will help you locate prep courses in your area to prepare for college admission exams.

CAREERS AND MAJORS

STEM Jobs www.stemjobs.com/ - website dedicated to promoting STEM education. Great "find your STEM type" survey for students to explore options.

MyMajors http://www.mymajors.com/ - website dedicated to help students decide on a major by completing a short assessment. Students will receive a report with possible options.

Big Future by The College Board
www.bigfuture.collegeboard.org/explore-careers - Helps you explore/search possible majors based on career interests.

STUDY SKILLS

HowToStudy.com is designed to help students take control of their studies and get the most out of their education. Whether you're studying in a traditional or online program, you'll find valuable insider tips from experienced educators.
http://www.howtostudy.com/

OPPORTUNITIES

Posse

This program matches minority students that go to college together so they can keep track of each other. It specifically helps small liberal arts schools without a lot of diversity. Posse pairs people up to support each other in these environments.
PosseFoundation.org

QuestBridge

This is a non-profit program that links high-achieving low-income students with educational and scholarship opportunities at leading colleges and universities all over the United States.
Questbridge.org

DoSomething.org

This is one of the largest organizations for young people and social change in the world. It provides great opportunities for community service endeavors.

Verdel A. Jones

About the Author

Verdel A. Jones is a master educator who has spent more than twenty years sharing the information she learned as a teacher, counselor and district administrator in the state of New York, with members of her community. She has personally visited hundreds of college campuses and holds extensive knowledge about the higher education selection process. Her knowledge of the college exploration and selection process; current educational issues plus firsthand knowledge about the social and emotional challenges students experience, make her unique as an author on this topic.

However, she describes herself as a teacher at heart. For that reason, she has passionately shared timely and relevant information in her areas of expertise through radio and television programs. She is the producer and host of All About Us (AAU) Conversations with Verdel Jones TV and Conversations with Deli Radio. She bases her success on setting high expectations for every endeavor, which is why this book will provide such a wealth of information to the people who read it.

Verdel has earned two master's degrees. She holds one in educational leadership from Long Island University and another in secondary education from Hofstra University. She received her bachelor's degree in business administration from the University of Massachusetts, Boston.

WWW.DELITEACH.COM

CPSIA information can be obtained
at www.ICGtesting.com
Printed in the USA
BVOW11s0538080816
458199BV00007B/14/P